'Celia Bowring, one of the most influential women leaders in the evangelical world in the UK, has struck a powerful chord. Sensitive, encouraging, insightful and sometimes humorous – this poignant publication should be in the hands of everyone who serves alongside their spouse in ministry.'
**John Glass, Elim Pentecostal Churches**

'Celebrating the uniqueness of each of us, Celia manages to cover topics in a candid and practical style, which will make the reader think, laugh and cry. This is a must-read for all those in leadership and for those who care about them.'
**Killy and J.John, The Philo Trust**

'A book I would liked to have read 30 years ago at the beginning of our ministry. Full of wisdom for the often perplexing situations so many face in our everyday lives and ministries as women living with leadership ... Self-revealing ... open sharing of highs and lows, joys and sorrows, strengths and weaknesses in a godly and inspirational spectrum of life.'
**Marti Green, wife of Lynn Green, International Chairman of Youth With a Mission**

'This is a book which has been crying out to be written and Celia and her friends are richly qualified to address the theme of living with leadership. The book combines spiritual wisdom with some down-to-earth practical advice drawn from the diverse experiences of those who have lived with leadership. Listen to the voices of this book and I guarantee you will be encouraged in your own ministry.'
**David Coffey, Baptist World Alliance**

'Often humorous, sometimes heartbreaking, always honest – in this book the writer draws on the experiences of a wide range of

women married to Christian leaders. With a mixture of common sense, spiritual wisdom and unfailing sensitivity, she takes us on an uplifting but realistic exploration of all facets of life in "ministry". This long awaited book will be a valuable resource both for all those already married to Christian leaders and for those about to enter "ministry life."'
**Judy Wright, wife of the Principal, Spurgeon's College**

'This book of reports and reflections from the challenging coal face of ministry is a most useful tool for the spouse of every Christian leader. It helps to know you are not alone!'
**Biddy and Martin Turner, Superintendent Minister at the Methodist Central Hall, Westminster**

'If you are married to a leader *We're in this Together* is a must-have. The stories of leader's wives are woven together to provide a rich source of experience, insight and understanding along with helpful principles and lots of encouragement. We wish we'd had the benefit of this excellent resource 25 years ago!'
**Rachel Tween, teacher and wife of Nigel Tween, Principal, Regents Theological College**

'We feel this book is long overdue. If you are married to a church leader, you will find hope, health, humour and help in these pages. It is practical, biblical and truthful and may just take you into a better future more prepared.'
**Anona and Gerald Coates, speakers, authors, Pioneer**

I weave into my life today
The presence of God upon my way;
I weave into my life this hour
The mighty God and all his power.
I weave into my sore distress
His peace and calm and nothing less.
I weave into my steps so lame
Healing and helping of his name.
I weave into the darkest night
Strands of God – each shining bright.
I weave into each deed well done
Joy and hope of the risen Son.

(Anon)

# We're In This Together

## Living with Leadership

Celia Bowring

12 11 10 09 08 07 06 7 6 5 4 3 2 1

First published 2006 by Authentic Media
9 Holdom Avenue, Bletchley, Milton Keynes, Bucks, MK1 1QR, UK and
129 Mobilization Drive, Waynesboro, GA 30830-4575, USA
www.authenticmedia.co.uk
Authentic Media is a division of Send the Light Ltd, a company limited by guarantee (registered charity no. 270162)



**British Library Cataloguing in Publication Data**

A catalogue record for this book is available from the British Library

ISBN 1-85078-672-0

Scripture quotations are taken from the NEW INTERNATIONAL VERSION; NEW LIVING TRANSLATION; NEW KING JAMES VERSION; J.B. PHILLIPS; NEW LIVING BIBLE and THE MESSAGE

Cover design by 4-9-0 design.
Print Management by Adare Carwin
Typeset by GCS, Leighton Buzzard
Printed in Great Britain by J.H. Haynes and Co., Sparkford

# Contents

# Acknowledgements and Thanks

I could not have written this book without the loving support and encouragement from a number of dear friends.

Thank you to every single person (there were 458 of you!) who took the time and trouble to complete and return the questionnaires that supplied the information found in Appendix 1. Many added further interesting and helpful comments to their answers. But just imagine the effort involved in collating this vast number of replies to put the results together! I asked God long and earnestly for an angel to help me with this task, which I rapidly realised was beyond my own ability. He sent two to rescue me! Heather Stockwell and her husband Robert devoted many hours to this and I am indebted to them for their kindness, their prayers and for undertaking the work so carefully and accurately.

I believe the insights and stories of other contributors to the book, coming from a wide variety of backgrounds, ages and personal circumstances greatly enhanced it. Thank you to each one who willingly shared in this way, whether anonymously or under your own name. Almost all of you have been involved in some way in the ministry of 'Living with Leadership' over the years and have taught me so much about what it is like to be married to a Christian leader. I should also like to mention my dear friend Ruth Calver who, with Hazel Barclay, began LWL.

Thanks go to Diana Archer, Killy John and Christine Perkin who kindly read the manuscript and made excellent suggestions. Also to Sheila Jacobs, my editor at Authentic who demonstrated much patience and skill as she tidied up innumerable details, corrected mistakes and helped to shape the book into its present form.

I have already mentioned Christine Perkin and want to thank her also for writing the Preface. She and I worked very happily together for several years in 'Living with Leadership' and our friendship has been a life-saver to me on many occasions. Thank you, my friend, for everything.

Finally, thank you Lyndon for all the love, partnership and great fun we have enjoyed 'in this together' for all these years. Apart from knowing Jesus, meeting and marrying you is the very best thing that ever happened to me! And thank you for encouraging me to write this book and for all the help and back-up you gave to make sure I actually finished it.

*Celia Bowring*
*September 2005*

# Contributors

Diana Archer, Alison Atkinson, Anne Balfour, Pam Bendor-Samuel, Peggy Buchanan, Vicky Calver, Alison Ceaser, Helen Clarke, Anne Coles, Jarrod Cooper, David Crabb, Carina Craib, Jackie Cray, Julia Derbyshire, Pat Field, Christine Freeland, Beth Fudge, Janet Gaukroger, Marilyn Glass, Ruth Haslam, Michele Hawthorne, Audrey Hensman, Davina Irwin-Clark, Killy John, Susan Killick, Lou Kirk, Ellie Leighton, Cathy Madavan, Hazel Marchment, Lindsay Melluish, Rosie Payne, Dianne Parsons, Cynthia Peppiatt, Christine Perkin, Fiona Perry, Sarah Potter, Judith Saunderson, Sheila Shersby, Diane Taylor, Susanna Thomas, Sally Thompsett, Susan Trudinger, Marion White, Sue Wilmot, Judy Wright.

# Preface

I have so enjoyed working alongside Celia in the ministry of LWL over these past fifteen years. She has been the most wonderful colleague – fun, wise, real and brave. This book is born out of her commitment and understanding of women living and working alongside their husbands in full-time Christian ministry. LWL began back in the mid-eighties when there was a crying need to support and affirm women in this very particular role. Things have changed considerably since then; and in January 2005 we both felt, almost simultaneously, that God was saying we should lay down this ministry. Celia's vision in writing this book was to write down some of what we'd learnt over the years as we've met with women all over the country. She has brought together so much of what we heard and experienced; and I believe this book will be a wonderful resource and great encouragement to many women in the coming years.

*Christine Perkin*
*September 2005*

# Introduction

This is a book about, by and for women who are married to Christian leaders – in both local and parachurch ministries. I have wanted to write it for some time, to highlight some of their issues and share some of their views and experiences. Needless to say these women have their own identity, work, gifts and ministries quite apart from their husbands and I want to say straight away that this book doesn't seek to cast anyone into any one-size-fits-all clergy-wife mould. Individual circumstances and the way we are each uniquely fashioned by God with wide-ranging experience, perceptions and opinions mean we are all so different.

Over the last 30 years, roles and the opportunities have become more varied and influential. Increasingly, women are being ordained themselves, bringing about the new persona of 'the vicar's husband'. Others lead alongside their husbands in partnership 'up-front' or fulfil a supportive behind-the-scenes, role. Many follow their own careers, interests and ministries and neither expect nor wish to hold any position in their local church simply by virtue of being married to its leader. Some are adjusting to the fact – maybe with a sense of shock – that although the man they married was a teacher, a builder or a businessman, he has since entered the Christian ministry.

From the late eighties until 2005 I was involved in 'Living with Leadership'. This interdenominational ministry and network for leaders' wives operated for nearly twenty years, organising regional events and setting up local groups for prayer, friendship and relaxation where women could support one another. Through this I have had the privilege of meeting hundreds of women engaged in all sorts of ministries alongside their husbands. I have heard some fascinating stories: amazing answers to prayer, hard times, faith-stretching circumstances, great encouragement and joy, and occasionally deep unhappiness. Some of their experiences are included in this book, either anonymously, details altered to protect privacy, or identified by the writer's name.

*We're in this together* describes their lives, highlighting concerns, passing on wisdom and expressing something of how it really feels, on the inside, to be married to a Christian leader. It draws on the experiences of about fifty friends and others who kindly put pen to paper – or fingers to keyboard – and sent me their thoughts. Living with Leadership surveyed almost five hundred women married to men in local and parachurch leadership and many of these findings and responses are also included in this book. These 'voices' bring many different views and experiences to add to my own and I am so grateful to each person who took part.

Whether you have been 'living with leadership' for many decades or are just starting out, I hope and pray that this book will encourage and inspire you. As the title says, *We're in this together*; with our husbands and families, exercising gifts and ministries in various roles and making the journey side by side with Christ. We also have each other. When I meet another woman married to a church leader there is a sense of shared understanding and the possibility of confidentiality and trust. We can do so much to encourage one another.

> Let us hold unswervingly to the hope we profess, for he who promised is faithful. And let us consider how we may spur one another on towards love and good deeds. (Heb. 10:23,24, NIV)

families, [illegible] and [illegible] rites and making the journey side by side with Christ. We also have each other. When a [illegible] partner woman married in a church [illegible] there is a sense of shared understanding and the possibility of [illegible], and that we can [illegible] one another.

> For we hold [illegible] the hope we profess [illegible] promised is faithful. And let us consider how we may spur one another on toward love and good deeds. (Heb. 10:23–24 NIV)

# 1. Great Expectations

> Be yourself. You have gifts and callings God has given to you. Say 'no' to things that others try to place on you – their expectations of who you should be and what you should do. His yoke is easy and his burden is light. (Anon)

The following story is told by Helen Clarke – married to Ken, Bishop of Cavan, Church of Ireland.

> 'And you, Madam?' inquired the young receptionist as my husband and I checked into a city hotel late one night. His expression was one of bewilderment; he glanced in my direction as he repeated the question, followed by, 'Are you together sir? Will you be sharing the same room?' Ken, never known to miss the opportunity of enjoying such a moment, replied, 'Yes, we will be sharing a room tonight, thank you.' We realised the receptionist had assumed that my bishop husband belonged to another (celibate) denomination and was horrified to meet a religious leader who was falling into sin in such a public way. When we arrived in our room tired out after a day of travel and meetings we enjoyed the joke, and recalled a similar moment when travelling in the USA. Having rushed straight to the airport from a cathedral service we

> were relaxing in the departure lounge. After a while we became aware of an elderly gentleman who had his eyes fixed on Ken. When he could contain his curiosity no longer the gentleman came across to Ken, ignoring me, and asked in a loud American accent, for all present to hear: 'Are you a bishop, sir?' 'Yes,' Ken replied, 'why do you ask?' 'Oh! Usually a bishop would travel with two nuns; but you seem to have just the one!'

Perhaps you've been in a situation where someone is surprised to learn who you are married to and heard them saying something like 'Well, I wouldn't expect you to say (or do/wear/go to/laugh at/approve of) that – being a vicar's wife!' Sometimes, just finding out who you are can send a casual acquaintance into a mild panic, as they rapidly rewind the previous conversation in their minds to censor it for anything they said that could be construed as remotely rude or irreligious! Sometimes it can be rather tempting to break out of the stereotype and do something slightly shocking!

Lyndon and I have been married for 31 years. When we met he was training at London Bible College (now London School of Theology). In 1972 he was appointed to Kensington Temple, an Elim church, to assist Eldin Corsie – my first pastor, who led me to Christ. Lyndon and I worked very happily at 'KT' for ten years; we learned a great deal, made many lifelong friends and grew in faith and experience. Then we faced a crossroads in our lives. First of all we offered ourselves to serve as Elim missionaries in Tanzania – but that clearly was not 'it'. So Lyndon took on the role of coordinating local church evangelism throughout London which entailed us travelling to a different part of the city every Sunday. Gradually the way ahead became clear, and when the opportunity arose to be involved in the work of CARE Trust, we were both convinced that God was leading us into this parachurch ministry. It was very different from the direction we had expected our lives to go, but has proved to be exciting, stretching and most of the time great fun.

## The things we hope for

> Now faith means that we have full confidence in the things we hope for, it means being certain of things we cannot see. (Heb. 11:1, J.B. Phillips)

Our greatest expectation is that one day 'we shall be like him, for we shall see him as he is' (1 Jn. 3:2, NIV). For me this is 'the crunch'. I believe that without this breathtaking anticipation of eternity (even if most of the time it's just encouragingly in the back of our minds), we'd be empty of vision, as on the average day the certainty of heaven is probably quite remote from our ordinary perspective. Our Christian hope rests on believing that Jesus has redeemed our past, brought us to today and will be there for us forever. Paul wrote that without belief in the resurrection we are 'to be pitied more than all' (1 Cor. 15:19, NIV) and need this foundation of faith in a living, promise-keeping God, who will always walk with us and help us over every kind of terrain. Without it, Christian ministry would be a daunting prospect, so maintaining and deepening our relationship with Jesus will be a high priority for us.

It is a huge privilege to be involved in church leadership – or other forms of service that we may describe as 'being in the ministry'. The survey (see Appendix 1 for full details) reflected an overwhelming feeling that 'serving the Lord, being part of what he is doing in people's lives, seeing them come to Christ and grow in him ...' was what most women valued most. Many said being married to a church leader gave them great opportunities to develop their own gifting and ministries and was potentially hugely rewarding; a great adventure – but one chequered with tests and trials that sometimes proved to be severe. We may lose heart, especially when people misrepresent or misunderstand us, but keeping focused on our expectation of the main event – his kingdom coming and his will being accomplished – will carry us through.

## How others look at us

When it came out in 1992, Joanna Trollope's novel *The Rector's Wife* (Black Swan, 1992) caused quite a stir. It tells the story of Anna, who has been married to an Anglican clergyman for 20 years, living on very little in an unprepossessing house. All this time she has worked hard to do her duty: cooking, organising, delivering parish magazines and keeping her husband's surplices cleaned and pressed. Life becomes even more stressful when her husband is passed over for promotion and her daughter suffers from school bullies. At this point Anna rebels. She takes a job in the local supermarket and does all she can to regain a sense of self-worth – much to the horrified disapproval of the congregation and the anger of her husband. I think this book is worth reading, but interestingly the whole dynamic of a living faith is absent from it. I am glad that the reality is much more positive for the vast majority of ministers' wives – although I suspect many of us would identify with some aspects of Anna's situation.

Although most of the people we meet will accept us for who we are, there are a few who regard the

Christian community and the clergy in particular, as a group of holier-than-thou, other-worldly, worthy and rather boring anachronisms from another age and of little relevance in today's society. It can be frustrating to be misrepresented and caricatured like this.

In her book *Who'd be a Minister's Wife?* (Christian Focus, 2002) Heather Tinker writes

> For some reason clergy and their families are not regarded as normal human beings. As children cannot imagine teachers having a normal life outside school, so it seems that clergy families are not thought to be normal either. When one of my sons was eight years old, his school friends seriously thought that we all slept on the pews in church! Once when I offered a mother to drop in for coffee at my house, she said, 'Oh, I don't think of it as your home, I think of it as the vicarage' ... A young lady once said to me, when my husband was not in church because he had 'flu, 'you don't think of the vicar being ill, do you?'

Amazing aren't they? – other people's expectations! However, we may be able to take great advantage of others' curiosity and be a bridge between them and Christ. We can help people realise that we are actually very normal, and very likely face the same minor irritations and major traumas as they do. Once they get past the stodgy minister's wife caricature and discover someone who's fun to be with and ready to show interest and offer help when needed, who knows how God may work through us into their lives? The following account from one of the questionnaires we sent out when researching this book, echoes the experiences of many others who are able to share Christ with the people who are brought to their door.

We had only arrived at the church a few weeks earlier and I decided to invite a couple of mums I'd got friendly with at the school gate back for a coffee. They were intrigued to see the inside of 'a vicar's house'. 'What does your husband do all day?' she asked. 'Well, lots of things – but one of them is praying about people's troubles,' I answered, praying hard myself under my breath. At this, the woman burst into tears and began to share what had been happening to her. God began to really move in her life and soon she was signed up to do Alpha, bringing four of her friends along with her.

## Expectations from the church

Sometimes congregations have unrealistic hopes when a new vicar or minister arrives. A young woman I met at a Living with Leadership day some years ago asked my advice. The deacons of the small rural chapel where her husband was taking up his first job had described the previous minister's wife. Apparently this paragon had not only led the Tuesday afternoon Sisterhood Bright Hour, kept the church kitchen spotless and organised essential rotas for flower arranging, coffee making, crèche duty and newsletter distribution, but had also, single-handedly, run the Sunday school. As her successor, would she, the diaconate wondered, be happy to carry these ministries on? The new minister's wife, who had two small children, felt a little pressured to say the least! She was rather overwhelmed by all this expectation, knowing she'd have her work cut out settling the family in, supporting her husband and just finding her own feet in this new environment. What to do? 'Please say "no"!' I urged. 'Tell them politely and firmly that you want to wait at least six months before committing yourself to anything whatsoever. By then you will be in a better position to know what God wants you to do. And they are not so likely to take what you do for granted.'

Another woman describes how she did this

> In one parish the previous vicar's wife had run the Brownies, the Sunday school, Young Wives, Old People's Group and raised money through jumble sales. I arrived with four small children and said I wouldn't run anything!

As the family grew older however, she immersed herself in many kinds of ministry.

New Testament teaching requires high standards for those in Christian leadership. 1 Timothy 3 says

> It is a true saying that if someone wants to be an elder he desires an honorable responsibility. For an elder must be a man whose life cannot be spoken against. He must be faithful to his wife. He must exhibit self-control, live wisely, and have a good reputation. He must enjoy having guests in his home and must be able to teach. He must not be a heavy drinker or be violent. He must be gentle, peace loving, and not one who loves money. He must handle his family well, with children who respect and obey him. ... In the same way, their wives (the word also includes women helpers or deaconesses) must be respected and must not speak evil of others. They must exercise self-control and be faithful in everything they do.' (1 Tim. 3:1-4,11, NLT)

Within the UK Christian culture, different churchmanship, geographical areas and emphases of ministry have a bearing on how much is expected of the minister's wife. Every denomination has its own traditions. These days, however, increasing numbers of married women are employed outside the home and are not available to give extensive unpaid time to work for the church. Others are studying, perhaps preparing to take up or resume a career after raising the children. On the other hand many of the New Churches take on the couple as a team when they appoint a new leader, sometimes actually paying her as well as him! Of course, the Salvation Army always ran on this principle, being incredibly forward-looking in its attitude towards the ministry of women. But there are a few congregations still going by the BOGOF principle – rather like a supermarket offer to 'Buy One Get One Free' – almost automatically expecting the pastor's wife to perform certain duties without question and even to behave in certain ways, although this is less the case now than in the past. For the most part leaders' wives today are free to decide for themselves the extent of their involvement in church life.

Thankfully there is much more liberation about than when the following was published in the *Baptist Times* 120 years ago. Needless to say, it was written with tongue in cheek

> The minister's wife ought to be selected by a committee of the church.
>
> She should be warranted never to have babies or headaches, or neuralgia. She should have nerves of steel and sinews of iron.
>
> She should never be tired or sleepy and should be everybody's cheerful drudge.
>
> She should be intellectual, pious and domesticated.
>
> She should be able to keep her husband's house, darn his stockings, make his shirts, cook his dinner, light his fire and copy his sermons.

> She should be able to keep up the style of a lady on the wages of a day labourer and be always at leisure for good works and to receive morning calls.
>
> She should be secretary to the Band of Hope, the Dorcas Society and Home Mission.
>
> She should make clothing for the poor and gruel for the sick.
>
> And finally she should be pleased with everybody and everything and never desire any reward but the satisfaction of having done her duty and other people's too.

Is there a ghost of this attitude today in some church fellowships? The issue of expectation certainly came up as a common concern for those participating in our survey. A quarter cited 'unreal expectations' of the church as something they found difficult.

## Who we are and what we do

Arriving at a place of knowing what God expects and wants of us is a deeply liberating experience – one to hold on to when roles change and our situation becomes less clear. And regarding others' inappropriate, sometimes downright bizarre, notions about us with fond tolerance because of this 'knowing' might help to free us from frustration and anger at some of the daft, unfair or even unkind expectations we come up against. One questionnaire included this comment

> I don't really find it hard – more amusing – when people obviously have preconceptions about what a 'vicar's wife' should do. I once had a classic comment made to me by

> a very dear lady (who means well) who said 'It's such a shame we never see you in a skirt.' In some ways I feel a sense of victory that I do not fit in with the preconceived role of a vicar's wife (e.g. I don't wear floral A-line skirts, do flower arranging and run the Mothers' Union). Perhaps others are cross with me because I don't do the things they think I ought to, but I believe that's their problem, not mine.

Jacqui Frost is married to Rob, an evangelist in the Methodist Church and a broadcaster with Premier Radio. In an interview in *Woman Alive* a few years ago she shared how she came to terms with some of the expectations people had of her. She married at the age of 20 and the life of a minister's wife came as a big shock. She felt the church had expectations of her that she couldn't possibly fulfil. She lost her confidence, plus three stones in weight and the ability to drive; she couldn't even open the door to people. She felt isolated – ministers and their wives being advised against having close friends in their church. Her husband saw she was unhappy and encouraged her to find a job. She worked in a supermarket and this helped her to regain her confidence – it was good to do something outside the church. (Interview with Jacqui Frost by Catherine Francis. *Woman Alive* magazine, 25 April 2001.) Jacqui later went into teaching art and drama and then started the Lantern Arts Centre in South London which has been highly successful in its work with both children and adults.

Pat Field, who lives in Jersey, has memories of expectations too

> ... frantically tidying up the lounge for a Women's Meeting one afternoon, and being rather horrified to hear my children telling some early arrivals, 'Sorry, you can't come in yet! Mummy is still hoovering the lounge!' On

reflection, *why* was I horrified? After all, they presumably hoovered their lounges and many of them had children too. I guess it was something to do with my concern about their expectations of me as the perfect minister's wife, which I was not living up to, and feeling somehow that I was letting the Lord himself down.

On another occasion, and a different house, I remember standing at the back door yelling at our boys to get off the roof of the car parked in the road adjacent to our garden. They were standing on it to reach conkers on the chestnut trees growing in our garden. Their logic? 'Well, they were our conkers. We just needed to reach them!' My embarrassment was complete when someone came round the corner of the house, and said, 'Well, Pat! It's good to see you've fallen off your pedestal!!' I wasn't aware that I was on one in the first place, but it made me reflect ... had I put myself there – had they? I'm sure God didn't!

Helen Clarke – the versatile lady from the beginning of the chapter who managed to get herself mistaken not only for her husband's mistress but also for his personal nun, speaks from years of experience

Having been on the ministry-life-road for what seems a lifetime, the whole matter of perceptions and expectations fascinates me. I grew up in a rectory and subsequently married into ministry life. Many make assumptions as to what we should do and how we should behave and they have their own perceptions of what a ministry-wife's role might be. Thankfully the 'buy one, get one free' mindset is changing but I meet many women married to men in the ministry who struggle privately with the strain of expectations.

Expectations – who raises them? I wonder if, at times, we place great expectations on ourselves that neither church members nor even God himself ever places on us. Thank God that he doesn't make stereotyped ministers'

> wives. No! He creates each individual distinctively, in his image, for the sheer pleasure of having a beloved child to be in relationship with him. His best is that we should know a deep sense of security in our identity in him – given to us in sacred trust. Whatever our past, however difficult the present may seem and whatever we face in the future, our confidence can be 'The LORD is the stronghold of my life' (Ps. 27:1, NIV)

Helen has for many years been the inspiration behind Living with Leadership in Northern Ireland – now based with CARE for Northern Ireland in Belfast. Her wise and caring concern for women across the denominations has been a lifeline to many. Although Living with Leadership's central London office has now closed, the coordinating group she began continues to arrange events and retreats for pastors' wives to provide a 'safe place' to be honest about the expectations facing them – which are often hard to live up to. Similar independent groups are also active in about fifteen areas on the mainland.

Anne Coles, alongside Lindsay Melluish, organises excellent day conferences and retreats for women involved in ministry through the New Wine network. Her husband John is one of the senior leaders of New Wine. She writes

> One of the greatest blessings to me personally as I arrived apprehensively at the door of the vicarage of my husband's first living, was the fact that the previous vicar's wife had not been heavily involved in the life of the church. She had certainly taken part but had not initiated or led anything as far as I could see, and so there was no particular expectation on me to do so either. It was as if the small congregation was holding its breath to see what, if anything, I would get up to. And I had

the distinct impression that they would be very grateful for any interest I might show in their church! So I could put aside any nerves about performing to standard, or keeping the show going.

Apparently no one had been inside the vicarage either. My predecessor had believed in the private sanctuary of her home. So the first time that the PCC was invited to meet in our lounge was an occasion of some curiosity and delight. I was making a good impression just by being there!

As I ploughed my own new furrow, did what I felt able to handle and became increasingly involved in church life, I wondered sheepishly whether I would not be so blessed and appreciated by any future successor of mine!

About a year later, it was my turn to be shocked by an expectation I had never realised would be there. I'm glad God exposed it. Because there had been little spiritual progress and very little visible church growth, my husband and I had initially been crying out to God to do something. He answered us by showing us that we were the problem; we needed to be filled with his Spirit. It was glorious; renewing, restoring, healing and it brought us into a new consciousness of the Lord's presence and love for us. Soon people started to join us for worship, and the best place for learning to worship freely and share the good news of God's power was in our mid-week meeting.

One evening as I was making coffee in our kitchen with a member of the home group, she asked me how I had entered into the experience of being filled with the Spirit. 'It all started when I realised just how sinful my heart had become,' I began, intending to relate how I had been so resentful, bitter and full of self-pity because the church had not 'taken off' when we arrived. But my eye caught her look of horror, before I could continue. 'Are you all right?' I inquired. 'Oh yes, she muttered, 'only I suppose I never thought that a vicar's wife could be sinful' ... Now it was my turn to be horrified and

> declared somewhat defensively, 'I'm exactly the same as everyone else.' Since then I've tried to be open about my difficulties and struggles, so that I can avoid being put on a pedestal.
>
> However, the pedestal will always be a temptation and it's one that has to be fought off. If I'm not careful, I can begin to live in a fantasy world where I'm much holier and more sanctified than the reality. Perhaps that's why I have children. They constantly bring me down to earth!

And after all, in the end, it's God's expectations that really matter most. We will never please all the people all the time and probably we are too hard on ourselves too. It might be good to take stock and think through this issue, perhaps with another woman in a similar situation.

## Some points to consider

1. Try listing all the areas for which you feel responsible (e.g. caring and supporting husband, career, children, housework, any groups you run etc. ...)
2. Who are the people who expect certain things from you? (e.g. God, employer, child, individual people, husband, Church Board, yourself etc. ...)
3. Where do these expectations come from? Do you know what these people expect of you or are you just assuming?
4. Which of these expectations can you dismiss and which are genuine and reasonable and – most importantly – on God's agenda?
5. Is there someone whose perspective and understanding you trust with whom you could talk through these issues?

# 2. Living and Thriving in the Goldfish Bowl

Take a day off. Get an answer-phone. Pray for care bears who will just love you and pray for you and your needs. (Anon)

## 'The fish tank'

A few years ago my husband Lyndon persuaded me to have our own aquarium. So off he went to buy a large tropical fish tank complete with all the necessary accoutrements and a riotous shoal of guppies, golden guramis and glowlights to put in it. We placed the tank in pride of place where we could watch the fish whenever we wanted. It was really relaxing, we'd observe every fin flick and comment to each other about how the fish ate, played and fought – we could even monitor their sex-life. They had very little privacy.

Tropical fish do not thrive if it is too bright as their natural habitat is shaded – if not downright murky. Unwisely though, not only did we turn the spotlight on them every evening, but unfortunately positioned the tank in a very sunny spot, so they were often unshielded from the light. There were soon problems with their health, and algae – extremely unattractive green slime, attracting slug-like creatures and mould. To protect the physical, mental and social welfare of the fish we realised they needed regular times in peaceful obscurity.

Life in the Bowring fish tank became quite dramatic at times, especially if we had been too busy for the routine maintenance needed to keep a healthy equilibrium. The inmates sometimes became quite agitated and stir-crazy, swimming frenetically from side to side or lolling listlessly near the air pump. I often found myself involved well beyond the call of duty: emergency rescues of baby Black Mollies victimised by a sinister Angel Fish, general clearing up of decaying waterweed, and occasionally the tactful removal of belly-up corpses.

Although it looked so attractive and there were systems in place to maintain the correct temperature, oxygenation and food supply, life could become quite complicated and even fraught in the fish tank. It required more attention than we had realised, and we felt quite bad about our failure to nurture our charges. In the end we decided to put the hobby on hold until a calmer stage of our lives came along, and gave our fish away to a more committed household.

## Household of faith

Most of the living-with-leadership women I have met over the years have described themselves as privileged and fulfilled to be alongside and involved with their husbands in ministry. This is also reflected in our survey, many saying that their situation offers faith-stretching, interesting and exciting opportunities and challenges; that it is rewarding to see God at work in people's lives and beneficial for their children to grow up in the manse or vicarage. But there are the demands of Christian ministry as well. The church leader's job is never finished and the stress of work often spills over into the lives of his wife and family in various ways.

I think the phrase 'life in the goldfish bowl' describes the experience of local church leadership rather well. Like it or not, the minister, vicar or pastor along with his or her family, usually comes under close scrutiny from members of the congregation, especially when the vicarage or manse is church property and functions as more than a place to live. Church leaders' homes are typically used for meetings, counselling sessions, small groups and social events. Many ministry families live 'over the shop', or at least very near to it which means they are readily accessible – with the foibles of normal family life there for all to observe.

In our survey, the vast majority said they lived in large or medium sized houses. Slightly less than a third of couples owned their property themselves – all the others lived in accommodation provided by the church or parachurch agency for which they worked. About a third of those in local church ministry lived 'very close to the church' and over half 'close by'. Most women (three-quarters of them) reported that their home was regularly used for church ministry – especially for meetings! Clearly many gallons of tea, coffee and fruit juice are consumed in the average ministry home along with a great deal of food. Hospitality is a major factor for most of the women we surveyed.

Sue Wilmot lives in Reading; her husband is the vicar of Greyfriars Church. She has organised gatherings of Christian leaders' wives in the area for some years and enjoys speaking and working in her new role as Development Manager with the Bible Society. She writes

> I think church leadership is an enormous privilege and we can sometimes get locked in to seeing the disadvantages, forgetting the wonderful advantages that many of our congregation would love to have, like: no worries about housing, mortgages and upkeep (unless we own a property I suppose), husbands usually around at key family time 5–7pm and being able to work together in the most important task in the world: sharing God's love with those around us. Our children have been wonderfully spoilt by lots of surrogate grannies, we have been prayed for regularly by devoted prayer warriors, and we are often the recipients of generous gifts. The one that most stands out to us is significant for its anonymity. Whoever gave it took great pains to ensure this was so and I look forward to thanking them in heaven! Every year while we were in a parish in London a black sack would arrive on our doorstep on Christmas Eve in which was a hamper filled with goodies for all the family – party poppers and chocolate tree decorations for our children, luxury jams, nuts and wine for us, each item individually wrapped by the donor. I hope whoever it was, was as blessed in giving as we were in receiving!

Cathy Madavan and her husband minister in a Baptist church on the south coast. They also feel much cherished and appreciated

> Recently while we were away on sabbatical our church refitted our kitchen and bathroom and cleaned the whole house. They put a big red ribbon for us to cut on our return, and lots of other treats, like welcome home cake, food, a cleaned car full of petrol and sweets! I could continue. What a great church! We are very blessed.

Living before the congregation is surely a positive thing; inviting others to emulate our Christian lives is part of what leadership is about. Paul wrote to Timothy

Be an example to all believers in what you say, in the way you live, in your love, your faith and your purity.' (1 Tim. 4:12, NLT)

Jesus came and lived amongst us – in very close quarters with his followers, sharing everything together with them. Many of us find that shepherding those in our care inevitably involves the giving of ourselves, welcoming and accepting people into our lives to some degree.

Coping with the stresses and strains of ministry in a busy local church can be quite a test though. There is a narrow line to walk. Being ready for just about anything and responding in a 'professional' way, doing all we can to help but at the same time being our own self and not just acting the part … I wonder if the following piece (written anonymously) rings bells with you?

The life of [a] minister's wife is so varied and full of extremes that sometimes you feel like you're on a roller coaster. One day we can be alongside someone whose loved one is dying of cancer and the next rejoicing over a much longed-for baby. One minute facing criticism over a decision in the church which has caused someone to feel hurt and rejected, and the next receiving a lovely gift of flowers because of the love and support a grateful church member has received during a difficult time. It can be exhausting but never dull or lacking in variety!

The hardest thing is the feeling of being watched by those in the church. I guess we all watch those in the public eye. We are intrigued by them and so it follows that some people are intrigued by us! So they watch what we wear, how we furnish our house, how we relate to our husband, how our children behave, what they wear, where they go to school, where we go on holiday, and to some extent they are influenced by what they see.

That is a responsibility and it can be difficult getting the right balance between 'not caring what others think' and being so over-sensitive that we are completely consumed by it.

## Open home

However, for some women, the expectation that the house – even if it *is* owned by the church – will be used for congregational activities, is a real problem. They feel uncomfortable about people traipsing in and out of the family home as if it were an extension to the church building. Boundaries need to be agreed upon and respected and this is particularly important for women already struggling with their role and unsure of how they feel towards their husband's calling.

Christine Freeland and her husband have been in ministry in Methodist churches for many years. She has always demonstrated an ability to reach out to people in the congregation, and has also done all she could to come alongside other church leaders' wives to encourage them. I have appreciated her wisdom and kindness to me personally on many occasions. She writes

> I have always loved keeping 'open home', but then, I have been the one to initiate that. (There have been times when my husband has desired more privacy!) It is quite a different matter to feel that one's space has been violated. Even then we need to check our reactions. I was feeling ghastly one day – in bed with a tummy upset – when the door bell rang. I ignored it but could not resist the temptation to see who was walking away from the house. I was filled with indignation when I saw a well-meaning but rather intrusive member of our congregation put

down her bag and start weeding our front garden! It took me some time to shift my attitude from resentment to one of gratitude in witnessing what was meant as a spontaneous and anonymous act of love.

Graham and Diana Archer actually started and ran a church in their house. In her book about this, Diana tells the story from the vicar's wife's point of view. Here she describes what it was like each Sunday morning

> Every week it was metamorphosis. The table had to be turned round, boxes of crèche toys readied, chairs moved into the lounge and study, and double doors opened between the two rooms. Then the sofas must be rearranged, OHP installed, guitar tuned, and sermon lost and found. Finally the kitchen needed to be cleared and cups put out. It seemed to go on for ever and we were always only just ready when the doorbell began to ring.
>
> Then the same needed doing in reverse afterwards and various mini-versions throughout the week. Yet still the wonder of what was happening gripped and inspired me even as we prepared our home for another invasion. It still surprised me that week after week folk would just pile in through our front door. ...
>
> Actually the breaking point was the carpet. That carpet, gloriously new and unlike anything we had had before. For a start we had chosen it ... plain and pale pink. It was agony watching it lose its glory. Shoes after shoes after shoes trampled it. They came, they trampled and our carpet began to die. It shouldn't have mattered of course. What was a clean, fresh carpet compared to the unexpected joys of lives changed and a church born? ... I was struggling to keep up with my side of it all. It just seemed that everywhere I went the houses were spotless, neat, organised and peaceful, while I felt involved in a perpetual battle to hold back total chaos ... I began to feel that I must look to others how my carpet looked to me.

Imperfect, stained, and in need of improvement. (Diana Archer, *Who'd Plant a Church?*, Christina Press, 1998)

## Protecting our privacy

Many of us know what it's like to have people from the church in and out of the house, and can affirm that over the months and years they leave it considerably more dog-eared than they found it. I guess it's all a question of balancing the needs of others with our own requirements for privacy, and time off in particular. Do you ever get that 'peopled out' feeling? Someone once quipped 'True hospitality is making others feel at home when you wish they really were'!

Many agree that it is absolutely essential to protect our privacy and give each other time, especially during periods of pressure when we go through stressful experiences personally, in marriage and with our children.

Lyndon and I started out in the ministry in the early 1970s. We were on a big learning curve and eager to do it right. Expectations and norms were different to today. We belong to the Elim Pentecostal churches and in those days rules were very strict. So as a young assistant minister, Lyndon was paid very little. In fact his salary of £350 per annum was exactly the same as the rent of the flat because our church was situated in the heart of Notting Hill Gate, an expensive area; there was no London weighting allowance to help us and at that time there was an archaic rule in Elim forbidding any church to help probationary ministers with accommodation. Thanks to the understanding and generosity of the Church Board a way round this problem was found and shortly afterwards we married and moved into a small top floor flat, able to live fairly comfortably on my teacher's pay and his minister's stipend (which they had doubled overnight!) We often had people from the church up for coffee, meals and various meetings, but guarded our time off assiduously. It is easier in a big city to protect your privacy and although our one bedroom fifth-floor attic home was hardly the proverbial Englishman's castle there were times when we could pull up the drawbridge and hide, able to enjoy just being ourselves, on our own.

Whilst many respondents to the questionnaire reported that they felt affirmed and taken care of by members of their church, many others expressed pain because of criticism and being taken for granted. Here are some of the comments we received in answer to the question: 'What do you most dislike and struggle with, being married to a Christian leader?'

One minister's wife commented sadly

> The church expects too much. I hope I'd never lose my faith in God but I sometimes despair of people and long to just hide away where they cannot make endless demands on my time and energy. The criticism and unrealistic expectations from church members, and having to go to church as what feels like a single mother.

Another said

> I have found it increasingly difficult to cope with criticism of Mike (not his real name) and his ministry and often with the disagreeable way people express themselves at a church meeting. It's such a fine line between holding truly to the vision you believe God has given and yet not thinking you have all the answers. How do you try to accommodate people's wants and needs without becoming a 'people pleaser'? I find myself incredibly tense and

> anxious and it really affects me physically as well. I want to support Mike but absolutely dread church meetings and have begun to wonder whether my presence actually makes it harder for him.

Killy's husband J. John is an evangelist. He is often away and when at home is busy writing and developing the ministry of Philo Trust. She writes

> For several years from the very beginning of our marriage the office was in our home, starting with a part-time secretary and ending up with four full time staff. The house wasn't really big enough for all the people and boxes of books filled the garage so in the end the office moved into separate accommodation. Having John work at home had both disadvantages and advantages; when they all moved out it meant a huge change for me, but the freedom we now have is superb.
>
> When we were dating I travelled the country visiting John at various missions. It didn't get much better when we were first married, 'Oh, you live here too' could probably sum it up! Over the years we have learnt the crucial importance of days off, answer-phone switched on, computer logged off. A Christian leader's life is not routine, weekends are generally hopeless, so my advice is to be creative and book in those elusive days off.

At certain stages sharing the house with the needs of the church may be more of a problem – and then wise restrictions may be called for to respond to family needs at that time. Teenage years may require this, especially if children feel resentful towards the church for some reason or other. This comment was very typical of those responding to the survey

> We try to keep family time; on days off the answer-phone takes all the calls and routine things will be left. We

> also use BT's 'call sign service' which gives us a second private number for close friends and family, which has a distinctly different ring tone.

Jarrod Cooper, now in full-time ministry himself as a songwriter and minister, writes very honestly – and humorously! – about his childhood

> I knew I was more important than the church. The phone could, and would be unplugged. There have to be moments when the only reason for disturbance is death. And if they want you then, they can come and get you themselves.
>
> Our home was not a counselling room. All counselling happened down the church. If people turned up at the door they could be turned away. 'No' was a very possible answer to a cry for help. Not always, but definitely possible. Even Jesus was purpose driven rather than need driven.
>
> I vividly remember my mum in a 'don't mess with me' mood walking up to my dad, who was graciously counselling some poor soul on the end of the phone, and hanging up for him. I guess the 'poor soul' outstayed his welcome (he had been on the phone for days, or so it felt). It was naughty I know, but the power was in the hands of the family. My parents were not doormats; they were stewards firstly of a family, then of a church. I knew where the lines were drawn, that, if push came to shove, a meeting could be cancelled, a counselling session postponed or a leaders' get-together missed. Why? Because my brother and I – in fact all of us in The Family were most important in the world.

They say that young children spell the word 'love' T.I.M.E. In my experience they would spell it many other ways besides but the principle is there; that relationships need the investment of regular, unhurried and exclusive time in order to flourish. By all accounts this is at a premium in many clergy households. Our survey clearly showed that they come under considerable pressure. The most common causes for stress were work overload, feeling isolated, criticism from others, financial pressures and uncertainty about their role. Out of the 392 people replying to this question only 25 said they 'almost never' felt stressed – and 14 described themselves as 'constantly' stressed.

Reading through the returned questionnaires, it was clear that a Sabbath rest was very desirable but all too often unobtainable. Most ministers' wives see it as a clear priority to minimise 'goldfish bowl' strains as much as possible, especially by making sure days off and holidays are properly planned and enjoyed.

## Some points to consider

1. In our home, which areas and rooms are just for us? Are there reasonable limitations in place?
2. Could we 'ring fence' private times when visitors are asked not to call and the answering machine deals with telephone calls?
3. If it is difficult to relax in the house, especially at holiday time, how can we escape? Do we have any friends with caravans, country cottages (or even Spanish apartments!) that they might lend us?
4. Are there more practical steps we could take – reserving dates in the diary well ahead for days off and holidays, making it known that these are times when we definitely will not be available?

5. Would it be helpful to have 'church-free' conversation zones; at family meals for instance, and in bed?
6. How can we create opportunities to be alone together just as a couple?

# 3. Being Myself

> My positive advice is this; to find your own calling and keep some space in your life for yourself – however hard that is. I planned time to escape for a quiet day but also for a keep fit class or upholstery. I found it great to go into a group where no one knew me and bang in nails to get rid of my frustration! (Anon)

I had often heard it said that snowflakes are unique, each single six-sided molecule with its own individual shape – but always wondered if this was really true. It is.

## 'The snowflake'

An American photographer named Wilson A. Bentley, from Jericho, Vermont, USA, was so fascinated by snow crystals that he amassed a photographic collection of them. Nicknamed 'The Snowflake Man', he claimed that he never found two crystals exactly alike. He spent his life photographing snowflakes and in over forty years from 1885 to 1925 he took several thousand stunning pictures through a microscope. He made this observation: 'Under the microscope, I found that snowflakes were miracles of beauty; and it seemed a shame that this beauty should not be seen and appreciated by others. Every crystal was a masterpiece of design and no one design was ever repeated. When a snowflake melted, that design was forever lost. Just that much beauty was gone, without leaving any record behind.' (www.snowflakebentley.com)

Every hexagonal crystal is designed to hook up with others, and these joined together form snowflakes of varying sizes and types. As the flakes fall they also interlock to create an extraordinarily smooth surface that covers all that lies beneath, forming perhaps one of the most breathtaking scenes in nature. Apparently snow isn't just snow, there are several types – the Norwegians have many different words for it.

Are we not much more amazing than these crystals of snow; created uniquely by the God who loves us, and united with others to be part of his church?

> For we are God's own handiwork, his workmanship, his masterpiece! He has created us anew in Christ Jesus that we may do those good works that God planned beforehand for us – that we should walk in them living the good life that he prearranged and made ready for us long ago. (From Ephesians 2:10 [paraphrase])

## Knowing myself

My friend Christine Perkin, who partnered with me in Living with Leadership for several years, is much-appreciated as a speaker, especially by women preparing for or already in, local church ministry. She and her husband Paul have worked in three Anglican parishes over twenty-five years. Christine shares very positively about the full-time ministry – at the same time being honest about some of the pressures involved. Here she reflects on our eternal significance to God

> Psalm 139:13–16 speaks of how God formed us before our birth: 'You made all the delicate, inner parts of my body and knit me together in my mother's womb. Thank you for making me so wonderfully complex! Your workmanship is marvellous – and how well I know it. ... Every day of my life was recorded in your Book! Every moment was laid out before a single day had passed.' (NLB)

This means that nothing that happens is insignificant. God will use all of it to mould our lives, to make each one different and distinct. Our past experiences have played a part in shaping us and if we believe he allowed them to happen then we must also believe that he intends to use them.

Rick Warren suggests there are at least five different experiences from our past that are worth looking at

1. Family experiences: what did you learn growing up in your family?
2. Educational experiences: what were your favourite subjects in school?
3. Vocational experiences: what jobs have you been most effective in and most enjoyed?
4. Spiritual experiences: what have been your most meaningful times with God?
5. Painful experiences: what problems, hurts and trials have you learned from?

We all have a distinctive combination of experiences, gifts and personalities within which we can learn to work. It's so releasing and exciting when we realise that God wants us to be different from the rest – in his eyes, each of us stands out from the crowd.

We are not 'off the peg', but a 'one-off designer special'! But we need to find what makes us tick – how we work best:

To help with this try asking questions like these

What do I enjoy doing most?

When do I feel the most fully alive?

What activities or situations make me lose track of time?

Do I like routine or variety?

Do I prefer working with a team or by myself?

Am I more introverted or extroverted?

Am I more of a thinker or a feeler?
(From *The Purpose Driven Life,* Zondervan, 2002)

Satan will try to steal this uniqueness from us, both by tempting us to *compare* our ministry with others and to *conform* our ministry to the expectations of others. Comparison must be one of the great killers of our own individuality and uniqueness. Two Corinthians 10:12 warns that when we measure or compare ourselves with others we are not wise.

I feel certain that we need to go for what we are good at, the things we love doing – not for what we constantly feel we ought to do. And there will always be '*ought to's*' in church life, like

I ought to run a mother and toddler club

I ought to visit Jean in hospital

I ought to organise the women's groups

Of course there are certain responsibilities in all our lives we don't enjoy but can't escape, but I feel sure that generally speaking God doesn't work according to the principle of 'ought to'. There will always be people in the church who do not understand us and will try to get us to conform to what they think we should be doing. Ignore them! The apostle Paul often had to deal with critics who misunderstood and maligned his service. His response was always the same: avoid comparisons, resist exaggerations, and seek only God's commendation. I was once given this piece of advice: 'Never give up your right to have God be the one determining what you do in the church.'

Recently I went on what was meant to be a working weekend with another vicar's wife and then as half the meetings were cancelled, we had a day and a half to ourselves. We talked non-stop – mostly about ministry stuff we were doing in our churches – and it was just so exciting to hear of the different ways in which we were working. We had such different gifts and abilities. She told me how she was organising a wonderful women's creative evening for Christmas – making wreaths, cards, candles and table decorations – and a short evangelistic epilogue to round off the evening.

> I was totally in awe of her putting this together (anything to do with dried flowers, oasis, wire, tissue paper? Forget it, I'm hopeless). I just couldn't do it, but it fitted exactly who she was – a woman with an evangelistic heart, organisational ability and wonderful creative skills. She was being herself and God was using her that way.

## Finding my place

Once we have an inkling about who we are, what we're good at and how God would like to release our gifts, the next issue is how to put it into practice. There are many different views about the role of the minister's wife and this is hardly surprising as we each have our own perspective and are operating in completely different situations.

Marilyn Glass, married to John, the General Superintendent of the Elim Pentecostal churches has been a minister's wife for many decades. She writes

> The path of least resistance when changing church or changing role is to try to emulate our predecessors. God has called us to be ourselves and stepping outside that truth is as burdensome as David trying on Saul's armour prior to his encounter with Goliath. I have come to learn that he has a path that is tailor-made for me.

A substantial number of wives felt it was very inappropriate for them to have a 'role' as such – other than being themselves and operating like any other church member – just because they happened to be married to the minister. Most of these women acknowledged the importance of supporting their husbands and being there for the children when his work kept him away. Different stages in life also affected the way leaders' wives saw themselves in relation to the church. One person wrote this at the end of her questionnaire

> There seems to be a lot of emphasis on finding out what is our role or ministry or gifts etc. when personally I feel we can get too concerned about these things rather than getting on with serving where there is a need. There

> are always plenty of needs around! I am content to be my husband's wife and support him, and am not really concerned about searching for my role, but hopefully am content to serve where there is a need.

Another said

> I do not see myself as an 'extension of my husband'. I believe firmly that he was the one called by God to be a Priest and that just being married to him does not make me a 'mini-Priest' too. However, as his wife, I believe my role is to encourage and support him in his ministry.

Some women have very specific and obvious giftings that may be relatively easy to apply through a role. Someone who adores kids and has great teaching and organisational skills is an obvious candidate to work with the children in a church. A musician probably fits into the worship ministry. Women with hospitality gifts will find many outlets for their culinary and welcoming abilities. In the survey, respondents identified 'what they did'. A great deal! Many ticked several boxes – especially indicating work with children, women and youth, hospitality, counselling, prayer and administration.

Some women are good at lots of things and may find it more challenging to see what their role should be. The danger here may be overload. Christine Freeland says

> It has always surprised me that as we have moved to new appointments my role has developed in different directions with widely different age groups, organisations, (church and non-church); sometimes with a high-profile ministry, sometimes in the background. The gift of encouragement was identified in my younger years and it seemed rather nebulous at the time but I guess God has planted me in

very different situations where encouragement has been needed.

Killy believes very strongly that her role is to support her husband J. John as he exercises his evangelistic gifts. This rarely involves much 'up-front'. Her setting is primarily at home with their family, especially as their boys were growing up, particularly with their dad so often off travelling. Killy's security of who she is in Christ and her positive attitude to their lifestyle has resulted in the family feeling very much part of John's ministry – knowing they are the most precious aspect of his life.

> It doesn't matter if you stay home, go out to work or become involved with voluntary work. We can waste so much time feeling guilty, devalued or feeling we need to justify to others our choices. Taking this verse, Colossians 3:17, '... whatever you do or say, let it be as a representative of the Lord Jesus, all the while giving thanks through him to God the Father' (NLT) and using it can change an ordinary day into an extraordinary one. It's not that anything different is done, but my attitude is changed. Attitude is the mind's paintbrush, it can colour a variety of situations.

Beth Fudge's husband Tim is a full-time youth pastor. Their partnership has undergone various changes as she has tried to find the best pattern for their ministry together.

> Tim has a tremendous vision and a real gift of faith. I don't! That's not a problem as it's not my role to head up the youth/children's work – my place is to stand with Tim and support him; pray for him, listen to him, provide a sounding board for his thoughts, ideas and dreams.

> However I need to make sure my lesser faith does not hinder his work in any way.
>
> In the earlier days (pre-children) I used to help Tim hands-on and we were seen as a great team – and we do work well together as a team, complementing each other. However there was a gradual move away from that which I found very hard at first. But I discovered that supporting Tim didn't necessarily need me to be there doing it with him. On the evenings when he was running clubs I saw my support role as providing a calm cheerful atmosphere before he left the house, praying for him and the other leaders during the evening and being actively interested to hear all about it when he returned.

Janet Gaukroger is a Baptist minister's wife in a thriving church in Buckinghamshire. A speaker and writer, she has specialised in providing excellent teaching and creative activities for young children in church.

> I serve the church because that's what I feel I should do, and I do so gladly and willingly. But each minister's wife must find her own way. The experience of being a minister's wife has been 100 per cent positive. I wouldn't want to do anything else if you paid me. Part of that is my personality, in that I've never felt any pressures or guilt about whether I'm doing enough within the church; but that says a lot about the churches we've worked in. They've been family.

I consider ministers' wives to be unsung heroines. Sometimes their role is behind the scenes, attracting little acclaim but vital for the successful functioning and well-being of the church. Others have developed their own ministries, through their work in the church, employment or other activities. 'Being ourselves' and finding out what it is that God has prepared for us to do will bring fulfilment and satisfaction – that we have built something that will last for eternity even if it is forgotten on earth.

## Being real

I have often reflected on a maxim of my father's. He always maintained that 'all experience is good experience if you know what to do with it.' All of us look back on painful memories, toe-curling embarrassments and guilty pangs about what we did or did not do; but it is now that matters, and how we will put our past to work tomorrow.

> He comforts us in all our troubles so that we can comfort others. When they are troubled, we will be able to give them the same comfort God has given us.' (2 Cor. 1:4, NLT)

Alison Ceaser and her husband Martin minister in a South London Baptist church

> After the birth of our third child, I suffered from post-natal depression. I did my best to hide it from the outside world, and tried to deny that it was happening! How could I, a pastor's wife, let anyone see that I could not cope with the simple things of life? After weeks of making my family's life very difficult, I decided to 'go public' at church, and was amazed by the response. That Sunday, many people broke down as they began to face up to their own struggles. It was as if they had been given permission to be weak and felt a release in knowing that 'even the minister's wife has problems'. I too felt that I was now allowed to be real, to be me. Of course, it didn't all end there, and I had a long way to go, but that was definitely a good place to start.

Sharing ourselves, modelling vulnerability, is risky but can be very powerful in God's hands. Lyndon and I have spoken together at many seminars – on marriage especially. To be honest I don't think we have many original things to say on this subject but on the occasions that we have been able to be honest about our own struggles, people have been deeply appreciative. How we live probably speaks more eloquently than what we say and often sharing our own hurts and misunderstandings gives others hope and encouragement to find God's answers for their own situations. I read this somewhere

> The most important quality for leadership is not perfection but credibility – and you build that not by trying to be perfect but by being honest. (Source unknown)

An earlier chapter looked at some of the expectations and attitudes that come across to wives of Christian leaders. Women completing the questionnaire overwhelmingly stressed how important it was to 'be myself', breaking free of any restrictive stereotypes, wherever they may come from. This might seem straightforward but in practice is not so easy to accomplish. Ministers' wives are in the unusual position of being in leadership – and yet not being in leadership. Merely by being married to the vicar or minister we vicariously experience the kind of stresses that come with responsibility – bearing criticism, taking important decisions, knowing confidential and sometimes heart-breaking information about people and situations. Any further role we may play in the church is in addition. This is not only true in local church ministry but also for those of us in parachurch work; in mission and evangelism and working with Christian organisations.

Sometimes wives find themselves grappling with the issue of their identity, especially when circumstances change, the role required of her husband is different and she is unsure yet how she will fit in. She may even be referred to merely as 'so-and-so's wife' rather than herself. One church leader's wife said this

> Recently I was at a minister's meeting where someone who knows both Mark and I introduced a friend to us. Well, if I am truthful, they introduced a friend to Mark. The friend immediately began a conversation with Mark and I became an invisible person who wanted to drag my chair across, stand on it and shout loudly – 'Excuse me but I am a real person too!'

John Pantry wrote a song more than twenty-five years ago that often comes to mind. The lyrics, about being ourselves in Jesus, and his being himself in us ('Empty Handed', Kingsway, 1978, UK. Maranatha!), remind me of Paul's words

> With eyes wide open to the mercies of God I beg you, as an act of intelligent worship, to give your bodies as a living sacrifice, consecrated to him and acceptable by him. Don't let the world around you squeeze you into its own mould, but let God re-make you so that your whole attitude to life is changed. (Rom. 12:1,2, J.B. Phillips)

Colossians 1:27 tells us

> And this is the secret: Christ lives in you, and this is your assurance that you will share in his glory. (NLT)

Our identity is wrapped up with Jesus. Not that we are subsumed into some huge cosmic being. No! In Christ we are gloriously liberated to be ourselves – the individuals in God's image he created us to be, saved through the cross by grace and made new through resurrection power.

The 'Snowflake Man', Wilson A. Bentley, lamented the fact that 'When a snowflake melted, that design was forever lost. Just that much beauty was gone, without leaving any record behind.' I so wish he had been alive today, to hear what scientists have since discovered. For apparently, if in the laboratory a single crystal is melted on glass and then re-frozen, it reconfigures itself in precisely the same shape – its beauty resurrected with the potential to live forever. So it is with us. We are made uniquely in the image of God and were made to be the way he planned.

## Some points to consider

1. It may be helpful to reflect more deeply on these questions, from earlier in the chapter – perhaps with a friend, taking turns to answer them together for each other.
   - What do I enjoy doing most?
   - When do I feel the most fully alive?
   - What activities or situations make me lose track of time?
   - Do I like routine or variety?
   - Do I prefer working with a team or by myself?
   - Am I more introverted or extroverted?
   - Am I more of a thinker or a feeler?

2. Am I 'free to be me' in my current situation? If not, are there steps I can take?

3. Looking into the future, do I have dreams and a sense of God having specific tasks and roles for me? How can I get ready for that?

# 4. Juggling Priorities

> Yes, our home is regularly used for church ministry. I am involved in many church activities – organising, leading and general up-fronting. We have four children aged twelve, eleven, eight and seven. I work as a part-time health service manager and go to the gym to relax. (Anon)

## 'The juggler'

In my dream, I watched mesmerised as the juggler effortlessly tossed flaming torches in the air and then with his other pair of hands began to spin delicate china plates on sticks which he then held between his teeth, then his toes and even balanced in one ear! I cheered and clapped as, coming to the climax of the act – now blindfolded, whistling 'God save the Queen' and seated on a unicycle – he added some daggers to everything else that was whizzing round his head. When he fell to the floor with everything tumbling on top of him I woke in a panic and realised the juggler was really me, desperately trying to keep everything in my life going against what felt like were all the odds!

It was the week before Spring Harvest and I was panicking that half my seminars were still unfinished. Inspiration for the one about 'Maintaining your spiritual health' was for some reason entirely eluding me and I soon needed to start packing for the five of us. I had an article to write by Friday. The laundry basket was overflowing and the ironing stacked high. School had phoned that day to report one of our sons had possibly fractured his ankle and needed to be collected and taken to A and E. We went and he had. Our daughter was going through a period of feeling emotionally fragile, needing unhurried tea and sympathy most days both when she came home from school and at bedtime. I had no idea what I was going to cook for supper. And Lyndon was still away preaching, for another two days. Whenever he rang home I pretended everything was fine – there was nothing he could do anyway until he got back, and by then perhaps life would have calmed down.

To be a successful juggler you need to keep your eye on several balls at once, coordinate their movements and stop them falling to the ground. You have to stay calm, keep the audience wowed and try not to break anything. I don't think I'm very good at it. Juggling like this doesn't sound a very biblical way to approach life anyway.

## Ordering our world

Jesus had everyone wanting his attention. There seemed so much he had to achieve especially in those three years of ministry when the crowds constantly clamoured for his teaching and the sick begged to be healed. He had a band of disciples to train up and a pack of enemies to deal with who were always trying to catch him out. So how did Jesus order his life with such a sense of calm purpose? Not with frenetic juggling. Jesus knew who he was and what he was on earth to do. He listened to his Father to draw strength from him each day for whatever task and challenge awaited. 'The Son can do nothing by himself. He does only what he sees the Father doing.' (Jn. 5:19, NLT)

This really challenges me, because when under pressure, I often go into high-activity mode. I act as if I believed it safer and quicker to rely on my own resources and strategies than to actually stop to pray – and listen. I suspect that many of us find it difficult to maintain a regular time to pray and read Scripture each day but the older I become the more I long to achieve this consistently, knowing that it will bear fruit.

Carina Craib lives in Glasgow, where her husband pastors a church. She sent me the following thoughts

1. You cannot please all the people all the time. Seek to please God and be obedient to him. Don't be a people pleaser.
2. Rejoice that the hard times bring us closer to God and are to make us more like Jesus. Don't battle against them.
3. The devil attacks when there is something worth attacking. When you are doing something right you become a threat.
4. God is ALWAYS faithful, and has already won the victory.
5. Criticism of a pastor is always harder for the wife.
6. Constantly ask the Spirit to give you more grace, forgiveness and love and don't let any bitterness or resentment take root. The enemy loves them.
7. Fear God not people.

8. Always be yourself, God made you that way. We have a responsibility to our husband and children before anything for the church.
9. Keep your heart soft. It may get hurt but God can use you.
10. When you find that he is all that you have, you find that he is all that you need.

## Unless the Lord builds the house …

Psalm 127 was written by King Solomon – presumably he was thinking of his great project of building the temple of the Lord in Jerusalem.

> Unless the LORD builds the house,
> its builders labour in vain.
> Unless the LORD watches over the city,
> the watchmen stand guard in vain. (vv. 1,2, NIV)

It is so easy to forget to ask God to show us how we fit into his plan. Eager to do good, we can sometimes rush impulsively into situations to pick up responsibilities and roles that were never meant for us. These 'uncommanded works' sooner or later lead to disappointment and dissipate energy. By contrast, carrying out what God has prepared for us to do is very different. Even when the way is difficult and the task demanding, doing something he asks of me – be it motherhood, writing prayers, preparing a meal or whatever – gives us the feeling of having the wind in our sails. The Holy Spirit gives us the anointing of wisdom, strength and grace if we ask, so we can do it well. The secret is to *know* what he wants and not get restless and worried about the other things we can do little about.

Jesus really understood us when he spoke about the anxieties people experience in everyday life. In the Sermon on the Mount he taught us that the principle of putting God first – trusting and obeying him – is the best foundation on which to order priorities. We can interpret that on various levels and apply it to the big questions of life and also small concerns and decisions that affect us today but may be well be completely forgotten this time next week. The people listening to the Sermon on the Mount had a majestic view down over the Sea of Galilee. When Jesus spoke of birds and wild flowers – how their heavenly Father provided them with food and clothing – the crowd saw them all around them. He reassured them

> Do not worry, saying 'What shall we eat?' or 'What shall we wear? ... your heavenly Father knows that you need them. But seek first his kingdom and his righteousness, and all these things will be given to you as well.' (Mt. 6:31–33, NIV)

*The Message* paraphrases what Jesus says here too

> ... you know ... God and how he works. Steep your life in God-reality, God-initiative, God-provisions. Don't worry about missing out. You'll find all your everyday human concerns will be met.

## 'The puzzle'

Cathy Madavan is married to Mark, a Baptist minister near Southampton. She expresses her thoughts about the many roles she fulfils like this

> I have a confession. I love jigsaw puzzles. And when I say love, you must understand, I mean love as in a compulsive

obsessive sort of love with slightly pathological tendencies! The Lord bless and keep those who dare to come between me and my little piece of cardboard (hmmm – I know I have seen the place for that somewhere!)

My toes curl with pleasure and excitement when the jumble of pieces begin to form a picture, and all that patience and trial and error finally begin to pay off.

I cannot help but smile as I consider that my life is some sort of puzzle. A picture, albeit unfinished and quite a muddle, made up of pieces. Each piece is unique and important, but alone is not complete. You have pieces like the wife, the mum, the leader, the friend, the singer, the part-time worker, the daughter, the speaker, the cleaner and the minister's wife (an odd shaped piece that doesn't know quite where it fits sometimes!). I think I can gradually see the pieces fitting together better, and the picture of me is getting clearer all the time.

Fortunately the hand that created the puzzle of me before I was born, is still shaping me. He really loves me, and holds each piece of me, not like cardboard but as treasure. Amazingly, he even loves the slightly odd misshapen bits of me with a passion – even those bits which I, in my great wisdom, rather wish he'd designed differently. I think my best bet is to put the pieces fully into his hands, and to stop thinking I know where they should be. He knows where they need to go. He knows the design, and what the finished picture could look like if it was completely surrendered to the Maker's plan.

So here I am today – juggling pieces as usual. With a dishcloth in one hand, a phone in the other, Barbies waiting to be groomed and the computer humming patiently in the background, I want to be all that God sees I can be, and to love and cherish each piece he has blessed me with. I long to have a heart like His that has time to see the beauty in the puzzles of other people's lives – they are just incomplete pictures like me after all.

And do excuse my over-active imagination, but I'm wondering if maybe, just maybe if I look really hard I will see his heavenly toes curl with pleasure and excitement as I slowly but surely sort out the muddle, arrange the pieces in some kind of order and try to live in a way that brings him pleasure.

By the way, has anyone seen that edge piece anywhere? The one with sky on it. I know I had it a few minutes ago. Oh bother…

## Changing world – unchanging God

I always find this prayer of Reinhold Niebuhr comforting and for years have kept a copy stuck to a cupboard door in the kitchen

> God grant me serenity to accept the things I cannot change; courage to change the things I can; and wisdom to know the difference.

Change is inevitable in all our lives; it can feel good and stimulating – the start of a new adventure – but is sometimes less welcome, forcing us from our comfort zones and making the future look uncertain. Change may come gradually and be subject to our careful planning, or suddenly, testing our ability to adapt quickly and wisely. It may represent success and celebration or it may indicate disappointment and displacement.

Anne Balfour is a clinical psychologist and has written about the effects of pressure and change in our lives. She and her husband, Doug, have experienced considerable lifestyle changes themselves too. A year after the birth of their first child they worked with Youth with a Mission in the Netherlands and then with Medair in West Africa. Some years later Doug became the General Director of Tearfund. Anne has been involved in the leadership of their local church for several years and was part of Living with Leadership's national coordinating group.

Anne and another psychologist produced a pack titled *Winning Under Pressure* and refer to a 'Lifestyle Inventory' – reproduced in Appendix 3. This scale illustrates how change can affect us, especially in the way that little things can pile on that feeling and experience of being stressed.

> A common pattern that emerges when people experience changes in their lives, whether they see that change as being positive (e.g. marriage, a desired promotion, a house move), or negative (like a bereavement and redundancy), is that it has an effect on them, physically, emotionally, psychologically and spiritually – and that effect builds up! That change may be an intentional one, a sudden surprise, or a growing awareness that you are moving into a new stage in life. But in each case a predictable cycle of reactions is triggered. This 'transition cycle' goes like this
>
> - *Immobilisation* – feelings of shock and being overwhelmed. A mismatch between high expectations and reality
> - *Denial of change* – temporary retreat from what is happening
> - *Incompetence* – awareness that change is necessary, frustration about how to deal with it
> - *Acceptance of reality* – letting go of past comfortable attitudes and behaviours
> - *Testing* – testing new approaches that may or may not work
> - *Search for meaning* – internalisation, seeking to understand why things are different
> - *Integration* – incorporate meanings into new behaviour

You may be surprised to see how many common feelings and thoughts can be symptoms of stress; whether these are physical, mental or actual ailments. Examples of these would be headaches, stomach aches, difficulty sleeping, frequent indigestion or constantly going for the chocolate biscuit tin! Beyond these physical symptoms may be feelings of failure, loss of interest in sex, difficulty concentrating etc.

Marilyn Glass (married to John, General Superintendent of the Elim churches) has faced considerable life changes: in her role, where they have worked, lived, and through health problems.

As our bodies and emotions mature over time and we seek to maintain control over our own destiny there will always be circumstances that negate our ability to entirely rule the route that our life will take. There are options that we consciously take but there will always be choices that are made for us and as circumstances will inevitably dictate.

At the point that I committed myself to marriage to a minister I was expecting a future that would catapult me into growth and change and, while not knowing the precise form it would take, was aware that there would be as many situations that I would find stretching and even daunting as I would find pleasing and exciting. Thirty-three years later I would like to say that I had embraced every transition with confidence – but that is not the case! Change has sometimes involved pulling up roots embedded in close friendships and familiar ties and moving to virgin territory knowing that growing true relationship, like trust, takes time.

Some people seem to take such things easily in their stride. Knowing this, I sometimes engaged in reprimanding myself for not getting it right: even challenging my own values and need for the familiar. This only served to exacerbate the problem because, as well as struggling, I felt condemned by my perceived inability to adjust. In 2000 my husband was elected General Superintendent of the Elim churches. We had been in pastoral ministry for all but a period of nine years and I had always warmed to the intimacy that was the essence of being part of pastoral ministry in the local church. Title and status were not the highest issues on my agenda.

I sometimes envied our two Siamese cats that adjusted to change with such ease knowing that they had warmth food and shelter and were happy 'just because I was around'. Whatever our status, or length of Christian service, in the end it all comes down to simple trust in the fact that there is someone there who cares and who is sovereignly in control.

Christine Freeland is no stranger to change. She and David have been in the ministry all their married lives and have now moved to 'retire' in Sussex – but I don't believe that for a moment. They have such a heart for people and will surely be sought out for advice and comfort for the rest of their lives!

The frequency with which Methodist ministers often move means that we should be used to it by now. Actually it gets harder and harder as time goes by; the physical, spiritual and emotional upheaval seems greater as does the length of time it takes, living hand to mouth until we really feel firm ground beneath us and a sense of corporate vision. And then it is time to move on yet again! Can this really be God's best for his church in these days? But then again, is this what it takes to keep us a Pilgrim People, when by choice we would not willingly embrace change?

Moving is never easy, especially when there are so many practical aspects to consider, but hopefully when we have to do it, the change will be the kind that brings progress with it. Julia Derbyshire recalls the painful upheaval she went through when her children were young and they had to move.

> I clearly remember the day my husband told me he had been asked to consider a move to another pastorate in a completely different location. We had been very happy for ten years and, for me, life was just beginning to change. My last child would be starting nursery school and I was looking forward to new areas of ministry opening up. I cried when I realised that this was indeed God's will for us. I cried again during a church service in our new church when I realised that there would be 'no going back'. We were staying and I wasn't sure I wanted to.
>
> Having to start all over again was very challenging and I felt I had regressed in some ways. I had no alternative but to trust and pray. Now, thirteen years on I cannot imagine being anywhere else!

After 21 years at Winchester Family Church, in association with New Frontiers, Greg and Ruth Haslam faced a radical change – moving to Westminster Chapel in the heart of London with its rich history of Dr Martin Lloyd-Jones and Dr R.T. Kendall. How did Ruth feel at that time?

> We'd been so happy here in Winchester and we were leaving a wonderful comfort zone. It was really tough to say goodbye but we looked back with such gratitude at all God had done. He had shown us clearly, in some amazing ways, that it was right to come to London. In the end I was very excited and felt at peace about it.

Change was not new to Ruth – she had adapted to many new experiences in her life.

> I grew up in Lancashire then came to work in London as a PA. When we married, Greg was a teacher and we'd no

idea that he would become a minister. I think there are two categories of ministers' wives: those who from the outset have a very definite sense of God's calling and the others who are there by default and wonder quite what happened. Certainly to start with I was the second sort! In the space of three months everything had changed. I left my job, we moved to Winchester (different to anywhere else I had ever known) and I became a pastor's wife. It was a steep learning curve, spiritually and in every other way too. First and foremost God trusted me with the responsibility to be there for my family; my prime role was as Greg's wife and mother to our children. As the years passed I took on various things in the church and loved it – especially leading the women's ministry, seeing them released into what God had for them.

Audrey Hensman and her husband ministered for many years in the East End of London. She recently wrote about how she felt regarding their move to somewhere very different

I think the biggest impact this time is the sense of being 'in limbo' – arriving somewhere new with no role, no friends (not yet knowing who might be a friend) and being introduced as 'the deacon's wife' all the time. It is lovely to have moved to the north of England, nearer to my roots, and finding the friendly northern attitude that I remember. At the same time, this is quite a socially self-sufficient community with lots of close family connections and established friendships, so overtures are not readily accepted.

It has also been strange to come into a church (a newly formed Local Ecumenical Partnership) with lots of folk who 'do things'. This is great, especially coming from a struggling East End situation where the Superintendent Minister held sway – but, again, no ready role for me to fill. Having said that, after six months, conversations are happening and ideas emerging ... [out of] my own experience that people might like to try, so maybe things will now begin to change quite rapidly.

Meanwhile, although I am volunteering with the Citizen's Advice Bureau, and not without things to do, it's still a lonely place to be at times. I think one of the most difficult things is knowing how to support a stressed, workaholic spouse who finds it hard to seek support and doesn't want to hear the obvious from his wife! I mostly adopt the tactic of 'letting him get on with it' but find myself embroiled at the least convenient times! That's life, I suppose, but 'feeling down' can be contagious.

## Priorities – what comes first?

What comes first? With so many demands from others, aspirations within ourselves and the day-to-day chores that have to be done, prioritising is an important issue. And what should come first this week may not be right next week. I believe we need to be constantly reappraising where our priorities lie but also determine which ones are timeless and non-negotiable.

Patricia Field says

> It took us some time to get our priorities right. We slowly came to realise that the correct order must be: God, spouse, family, church, and to begin to really practice it. The Lord did finally get us to do it and it is good to know his healing for the mistakes we made.

Rob and Marion White have been involved in all kinds of ministry, including teaching, pastoring, leading British Youth for Christ, and being key players in the annual interdenominational event, Spring Harvest. Marion has often had to review her priorities

Can you really balance ministry, marriage and the family?

The short answer is 'Yes, with difficulty, and sometimes only for short periods because balance changes constantly.' I think it needs to be viewed rather like a see-saw. Marriage could be a bit like the pivot in the middle with ministry/church at one end and the family at the other.

Most people I have talked to whose spouse is a minister or is involved in some kind of Christian ministry, say, that as a couple, they feel that marriage and family have a certain priority over ministry/church work but that in reality and practice it works the other way round!

Possibly this is because most ministers have a very high sense of calling and a very high expectation of themselves. Add to that the expectations of others and it is all too easy to feel guilty if they are not working at full pelt all the time.

I know the greatest gift is love but common sense comes pretty close behind. It is often in our own hands, particularly those of us who are spouses, to take practical steps to guard the people who are the most precious in our life – maybe doing simple things like turning the answer-phone on at mealtimes and children's bedtimes. When the children are little it is relatively easy to plan a family time at least once a week, although this is not so straightforward with teenagers as they often have very busy diaries themselves! If we work hard at our juggling skills our balance will improve!

First of all, prioritising involves putting life's major responsibilities in the right order. Relationships, job, caring for family and other non-negotiable ongoing commitments demand major shares of our time, resources and energy. Then within this 'big picture' are hundreds of tasks queuing up for attention and sometimes threatening to overwhelm us. As I mentioned before, stress is a major issue for leaders' wives – although anxiety does not always arise from the pressure to prioritise but is caused by other things too.

Jesus taught his followers to put him first – 'If you want to be my follower, you must love me more than your own father and mother, wife and children, brothers and sisters – yes, more than your own life' (Lk. 14:26, NLT) – but he was speaking more about heart attitude than lifestyle. Elsewhere he slated some religious leaders who refused to support their aged parents because they had no money left over from tithing to the temple. And his tender words for Mary uttered in agony as he died: '… he said to his mother, "Dear woman, here is your son," and to the disciple, "Here is your mother."' (Jn. 19:26,27, NIV) eloquently demonstrated Jesus' commitment to the family he loved so much.

These thoughts were added to one of the questionnaires and strike me as being a very representative view of ministers' wives in general, believing that family comes first.

> When we had children I believe it was my God-given job to make sure that I was always there for them and to release my husband to fulfil his ministry so he would have no concerns about their welfare. This was particularly important when he travelled to Africa for up to four weeks at a time during his first pastorate, when our children were young. Never did I feel that we were less important than his ministry and so it was easy to release him to go and do what he needed to.

I can really relate to this and remember Lyndon's promise to me at the beginning of our marriage 'to try and always to put you first. I believe my first responsibility before God is to cherish you and any children we may have in the future. If one day, I have to lay down the ministry because you need me to, I will.' I so appreciated his saying that and although it didn't always work out that smoothly I knew he meant it, which made me determined to support him as much as I could.

Most women are stunningly good at multi-tasking and usually sense when it is necessary to particularly concentrate on one person or responsibility. The survey showed that the issue of prioritising is an ongoing concern for many, especially at times when extra responsibilities come or we realise we have just taken on too much.

Personally I'm a great one for lists. They help me not to forget things, give an idea of what the coming day or week holds, reassure me that if something is written down it's as good as done and provide a sense of satisfaction when an item is ticked off. I confess to including things like 'coffee' and also writing down the jobs I hadn't noted earlier after they were done, just to make the list look longer, proof of how efficient and busy I am.

Susan Killick and her husband Barry have ministered in Elim churches for many years. She reflects on this whole business of juggling responsibilities, recalling a particular day in her life

> There are the practical things that need to be done; fitting in the baking of a birthday cake (or alternatively a quick dash to Tesco's to buy one!), sorting out papers.
>
> My brain is in overdrive. I've said yes to five requests despite knowing for sure that it will take a miracle to fulfil even three of them. It is futile to moan that I'm overloaded and constantly meeting myself coming back when it was me who said yes in the first place. When I sharply decline Mrs Bloggs' appeal for my assistance – she isn't to know that I've just negotiated myself through a minefield of eight day weeks without even stopping to

catch my breath. I need to learn to say no. If I don't there will never be time to smell the roses.

Perhaps the question of priorities really boils down to the relationships we juggle in our lives: in the home, at work, with our friends and family – and in the church. Relationships are of paramount importance in church life. There are many pitfalls to avoid – offending people unintentionally, getting involved with disagreements between others, avoiding unhealthily dependent or close relationships, dealing with those who exhibit signs of competitiveness or jealousy… Experience is our great teacher in these things but perhaps the following, given to me by a friend, might be a useful list to think about and perhaps talk about together.

## Some points to consider

*Ten Commandments of Relationships*

1. Know yourself and know others.
   - Study yourself. Know your temperament, inclinations, vulnerabilities and besetting sins!
   - Never practise 'scapegoating'! Recognise that most problems are 'in here' rather than 'out there'.
   - Try not to have unrealistic expectations of yourself or others.

2. Do not become a martyr over trivialities.
   - Some in ministry are bruised and battered unnecessarily over issues of colossal insignificance! Do not become one of them!
   - Very few issues are critically important – many fewer than you think! Recruit wise and godly

people to help distinguish the trivial from the significant.

3. Use words with restraint.
   - Remember: 'Even a fool is thought wise if he keeps silent, and discerning if he holds his tongue.' (Prov. 17:28, NIV)
   - Speak within the area of your competence. Otherwise, keep quiet.
   - You do not need to have an opinion on everything. Some that you do have may not need to be verbalised!
4. Be a listener; hear heartbeats not just words.
   - Listening communicates the most important message of all: 'I care about you'.
   - The most important things people have to say are seldom verbalised.
   - No one who is talking can listen at the same time.
5. Avoid the 'Junior Messiah' Complex – at all costs.
   - Be realistic about your ability to help people.
   - Do not attempt to 'fix' other people's quarrels. Do not let people 'dump' their personal problems on you.
   - Master the art of referral – otherwise known as delegation.
6. Do not react defensively to criticism.
   - Evaluate criticism carefully for whatever constructive value there might be; most criticism contains some truth – find it!
   - Feel free to ignore the criticism of perennial dissidents and chronic complainers.
   - Accept the reality that you cannot please everyone.

7. Never tie your plans and dreams to your ego.
   - When people don't take up or enthuse over your idea don't feel personally put down or rejected. The chances are that your idea was a poor one!
   - If your idea is rejected, support somebody else's, rather than sulk about the rejection of yours.

8. Do not speak about people in an uncomplimentary way.
   - If you have a criticism of somebody, take it directly to the person concerned.
   - Always assume that your uncomplimentary comments will be repeated word for word to the person concerned.

9. Play no favourites.
   - '... if you show favouritism, you sin' (Jas. 2:9, NIV)
   - Do not gain a reputation as one who 'hobnobs' with the socially desirable, i.e. the economically healthy, the young marrieds, those with a second home in the country, the 'beautiful people'.

10. Be transparent with people.
    - In whatever ways you can, say to people: 'This is who I am; I am human too, I do not have all the answers, I make mistakes, I struggle with the same kinds of things you do, I too need to be loved and ministered to.'
    - Use common sense in deciding the limits of transparency. If you don't have common sense, don't be transparent!
    - Recognise that there are appropriate levels of transparency. This depends on both the maturity of the recipients of your communication and the degree of trust you put in them.

*(Source unknown)*

# 5. Marriage Matters

Adam was hanging around the Garden of Eden feeling very lonely. God said that he was going to make Adam a companion – a woman. He said, 'This pretty lady will gather food for you, she will cook for you, and when you discover clothing, she will wash it for you. She will always agree with every decision you make and she will not nag you, and will always be the first to admit she was wrong when you've had a disagreement. She will praise you! She will bear your children and she will never ask you to get up in the middle of the night to take care of them. She will NEVER have a headache and will freely give you love and passion whenever you need it.' Adam asked God, 'What will a woman like this cost?' God replied, 'An arm and a leg.' Adam then asked, 'What can I get for a rib?'

Of course the rest is history… (Anon)

## 'The sailing ship'

A sailing vessel may journey over many seas – through all weathers, against currents, over dangerously rocky terrain and arriving in all kinds of harbours, anchorages and mooring places. She should be sturdy, built to last and designed to be a home to the crew and passengers living aboard together; sometimes harmoniously, sometimes not.

When constructed carefully, with the right materials and not in too much hurry, the ship should take to the water, eager to face the adventures ahead. The great launching ceremony comes with crowds of guests, champagne and speeches, a prayer for all who sail in her, and the honeymoon voyage begins. The relationship between captain and first mate – his partner in all things and often called upon to deputise if he is asleep, otherwise occupied or away – is crucially important. It needs to be based on trust, appreciation, respect and unity and if they really like each other that's especially good! As time goes on their understanding and tolerance of each other's characteristics and foibles should grow.

The art of successful sailing depends on several things. The captain and his mate (it's usually she who has more opportunity for this) each need to be aware of how the ship is 'feeling', conscious of each creak and groan of the timbers, the way the sails are flapping and straining, and the tension of ropes against the soaring masts and spars that carry the ship forward. Sometimes it will be necessary to do some pumping out of bilge water – and the interior of the ship should be clean as well as her hull and the decks. Those sailing her need to be going in the right direction; taking regular bearings and keeping in constant communication with the vessel's owner in order to receive up-to-date instructions and guidance. To ensure safe and accurate passage they require ample provisions, protective clothing, a compass, charts and a method of good communication with other ships and the shore. Sometimes there will be treacherous tides or violent storms to face and maybe even the possibility of shipwreck.

A ship at sea for weeks and months on end will begin to feel the strain. Regular maintenance and repairs in a safe haven are essential; for if neglected, small problems can expand into major crises, usually coming to a head at times of greatest stress endangering those around and those aboard. A longer quiet spell in a shipyard for full scale restoration work is also necessary from time to time – preferably in a peaceful, sunny setting!

'May God bless all who sail in her!'

## Rooted in Christ, sharing the vision

One of the most famous married duos in the New Testament – although tantalisingly little is written about them – is Aquila and Priscilla. They ministered with Paul, having been taught by him sitting cross-legged together in their tent making workshop in Corinth. Priscilla was a remarkable woman; strong, competent, professional and actively involved in Christian ministry in partnership with her husband. She is the nearest person I can find in Scripture to what we would think of as a 'pastor's wife.' However, the amazing tribute to the lady in Proverbs 31 is to me well worth revisiting, especially if I can manage to read it without feeling deeply inadequate! (In this extract from *The Message* I purposely left out some of the bits about knitting, needlework and buying fields!) Perhaps this chapter should be read out in our church on each of our birthdays, followed by the presentation of a large bouquet of flowers – and chocolates.

> *Hymn to a good (minister's?) wife*
> A good woman is hard to find, and worth far more than diamonds. Her husband trusts her without reserve, and never has reason to regret it. Never spiteful, she treats him generously all her life long. ... She's up before dawn, preparing breakfast for her family and organizing her day. ... First thing in the morning, she dresses for work, rolls up her sleeves, eager to get started. She senses the worth of her work, is in no hurry to call it quits for the day.

> She's skilled in the crafts of home and hearth, diligent in homemaking.
>
> She's quick to assist anyone in need, reaches out to help the poor. She doesn't worry about her family when it snows; their winter clothes are all mended and ready to wear. ...
>
> Her husband is greatly respected when he deliberates with the city fathers. ... When she speaks she has something worthwhile to say, and she always says it kindly. She keeps an eye on everyone in her household, and keeps them all busy and productive. Her children respect and bless her; her husband joins in with words of praise:
>
> 'Many women have done wonderful things, but you've outclassed them all!'
>
> Charm can mislead and beauty soon fades. The woman to be admired and praised is the woman who lives in the Fear-of-GOD. Give her everything she deserves!
>
> Festoon her life with praises!

It is a little difficult not to feel overwhelmed by this shining example of godly femininity! I don't know many vicars etc. who would pen such a paean to their wives but I am sure the majority of our husbands deeply love and appreciate us. Every marriage is different and no relationship is ever perfect, able to satisfy every need. But while close friendships with others can enrich us personally and bring fresh life into our marriage, it is great when we can say that our husband is our closest friend, and that that relationship is made up of many loves: companionship, admiration and respect, sexual attraction and romance – all bound together by our shared love for Jesus.

American 'ministry wife' Gail MacDonald, who is married to the well-known author and Bible teacher Gordon MacDonald, wrote an excellent book *High Call,*

*High Privilege* (USA: Hendrickson Publishers, 1998). In it she tells the story of their marriage and ministry together, through the rough and the smooth times and in the introduction describes this as a 'journey from being an "easy-answers girl" to a "fire-oriented woman".' Gail believes passionately in the important principle that

> it all begins with the fire within and your heart attitude … tending the fire within is another way of talking about being open to the presence of Christ … It takes time to come to the fire, it takes effort to keep the fire burning, it takes a willingness to become quiet enough to hear what God might be saying, and it takes courage to snuff out competing sounds and demands that attempt to shorten or neutralise the effect of the fire time.' (pp. 4,5)

She goes on to stress the importance of our personal relationship with God – that it must be strong enough to sustain us, confessing there was a time when this was not true for her in an earlier relationship before she met Gordon; when 'I was warming my soul on another person's fire, seeking a second-hand empowering, unfair for him, unhealthy for me.' She quotes Henri Nouwen

> No human being can understand us fully … give us unconditional love … offer constant affection … enter into the core of our beings and heal our deepest brokenness. When we forget that and expect from others more than they can give we become deeply disillusioned …'

I believe this trap – of relying too much on a spouse, and needing more from the marriage relationship than it can give – is easily fallen into. The best partnerships are between two people who are equal and complementary, learning to appreciate each other's differences and growing together. This is by no means easy!

Lifelong, faithful, happy marriage is God's desire for married couples, but in today's society this ideal is under considerable threat. In 2004, of the 17 million families in the UK; only around 7 in 10 of them were headed by a married couple. More than 160,000 marriages end in divorce each year, and one in four children live with a lone parent. ('Focus on Families' www.statistics.gov.uk) A growing number of countries grant same-sex couples the same status in law as traditional marriage. The practice of cohabitation is now common.

The church is in a position to model something else, when we uphold marriage as God intended – a vibrant, joyful union involving partnership at every level. It is a great thing that more and more couples now seek pre-marriage counselling and attend courses like 'The Marriage Course'(www.themarriagecourse.org) run by Nicky and Sila Lee, based at Holy Trinity Brompton (the home of Alpha).

So may God help us to guard these precious relationships, make our good marriages even better and pray they will be strong enough to recover from the various knocks life inevitably brings. In full-time ministry, marriage is on display; in many ways the relationship between the vicar and his wife authenticates his ministry – but it needs to be real, not on some kind of pedestal. Judith Saunders makes this comment

> Sometimes my view of my husband differs from that of others – for example a member of the congregation liked his latest haircut, and I didn't. They may see him as saintly but I may not – especially following a major argument. Somehow or other, people assume I have a degree in theology or have been trained to be a vicar's wife – especially to arrange flowers!

Judith, like so many others, is deeply committed to being in partnership with her husband in ministry but wants it to be clear what that 'partnership' means in reality. Sharing a vision in my opinion is fundamentally important in any marriage – identifying the family 'mission statement' – whether the couple is in church or other ministry leadership or not. How that core value is worked out is another matter, and the roles of each partner may well change throughout the years.

Many couples are opposites, which brings both blessing and challenge! A man may deeply appreciate his wife's ability to get on with people and oil the social wheels in the congregation, but at the same time become fatigued by her extrovert need to talk to him, often and at length! Lyndon and I are certainly different in many ways and 32 years into our marriage are still coming to terms with the implications of this. He is what he calls 'a tidy' who loves order (to me in my most grumpy moments, an unnecessarily fussy person whose priorities clash with mine). *I* am what he calls 'a messy' (or in my opinion a free spirit who loves to be spontaneous and see the big picture. And on those rare occasions when the family has run out of clean socks or something because I am busy on some project, well, 'worse things happen at sea!'). However we both agree on some fundamentals, among which are: that relationships are the most significant part of life, that hospitality is a must, and communicating truth in ways that make sense to people and help them grow closer to God is important. Sharing a vision and learning to live it out together is exciting – and often hard work.

## Time together

Love needs time and married couples who are able to carve it out to be together are more likely to grow – and stay – closer together. The survey underlined this; taking a regular day or other time off came to the fore as an important issue. Weekends don't really exist for couples in church leadership the way they do for normal people – even when the Saturday is free, it is overshadowed by the impending responsibilities of Sunday, the busiest and potentially the most stressful day of the week, although hopefully fulfilling and inspiring as well. Unless another day is set apart, the minister can find himself staying in 'work mode' all week; becoming tired, perhaps irritable and not spending much time with his nearest and dearest. I have met more than one woman who has written bogus appointments in her husband's diary in sheer desperation to get his undivided attention.

Marion White has led a very varied life alongside her husband Rob. They now travel together helping local churches and encouraging the leaders. It has always been busy – sometimes too busy – but Rob and Marion have always aimed to make time to nurture and enjoy their marriage relationship.

> Everyone needs to have a certain level of intimacy with a small number of people. Relationships need to have a good level of honesty and reality in them – a place where you can be yourself. The most important relationship in this respect is with one's spouse and on all levels this has to be worked at which means time and effort – often the most difficult [thing] to achieve. That extra 'spark' in our togetherness is attractive to others who inevitably see us as some kind of role model and is essential to save our situation from becoming mundane, routine and boring!

> Our children also need to know that their parents don't preach one thing and live another.

Beth Fudge recognised how important time together was for her and Tim early on in their relationship. This is what they do, and for the moment it's working well

> Tim works weekends and evenings as well as days. He therefore takes off the whole of Thursday. Although I have a demanding job myself I have made a point of not working on a Thursday. I was pleasantly surprised how understanding my boss was about this and Thursday is now our haven. It is vital to keep our marriage happy and healthy. We don't usually do anything 'glam', just walk for miles, talk, drink coffee etc. but in that time we share our hopes, dreams and worries. It is absolutely vital and keeps our marriage alive. We look forward to it as a light at the end of the tunnel especially if the preceding six days have been particularly demanding. We count Thursday as a very precious day: a day when we recharge our batteries, a day to be protected ferociously despite the temptations sometimes to do other things.

In the early seventies when Lyndon and I started out in ministry, Christians were sometimes urged to 'burn out not rust out' and spend every possible ounce of strength 'serving God'. When we requested one evening off a week, a few eyebrows were raised. Sundays were obviously non-stop and Saturdays got filled with weddings, meetings and other social 'must-go-to' events. Without our sacrosanct Friday evenings – and whenever possible the daytime too – we would have been in trouble sometimes. Our home was only five minutes walk from the church building and some people expected to call by unannounced, for counselling, tea, fellowship and goodness knows what else. But as our flat was on the fifth floor, we'd peer out of the kitchen window to check the identity of any visitors – and sometimes pretend to be out! We found there is something very special and enjoyable about sharing a meal together. Stick a candle in a holder, perhaps a few flowers in a vase and it doesn't matter too much what there is to eat if you're with someone special, at ease and with the prospect of some uninterrupted time to chat and enjoy one another's company.

From early on in our relationship, Lyndon and I learned to grab every opportunity we could to carve out time to be together. We are both inveterate talkers and need lots of time for catching up on what has happened and how we are thinking and feeling – especially when we have been apart for a few days. Without the opportunity to debrief, we imperceptibly drift apart, just a little, and lose track of each others' news, enthusiasms and concerns.

Our greatest treat has always been occasionally eating out. We had no children for the first eight and a half years of our marriage and the pleasure of sitting in a café or restaurant was just wonderful, even if we probably should have spent any spare money on more sensible things. Tucked away in Café Max, a cheap trattoria in the back streets of Notting Hill, we couldn't answer the phone (this was long before the days of mobiles) and wouldn't hear anyone knock at our door. We were anonymous, off duty and loving our plate of pasta. Sometimes we could only afford a bowl of soup and asked for extra bread and a carafe of water. The owner took pity on us after a while and showed us how to work the jukebox without using our 10p pieces so we could play again and again our song – 'Vincent' by Don McLean!

## Communication and intimacy

Time together helps to develop closeness but it is not an automatic result of it. The more we are able to share together about all sorts of issues and on every level, the greater our communication and the stronger our intimacy. One aspect of this is spiritual. Davina Irwin-Clark shares that she and Peter

> ... have always prayed together last thing at night. It hasn't always felt like a face-to-face encounter with God, but nevertheless we've prayed about ourselves, our marriage, the children, the ministry and always about our feelings and not just the facts of what's been going on. For a while, during a time of particular pressure, we carved out two hours on Friday mornings together. We'd walk in the New Forest or go out for coffee, and talk and pray at a much more positive and energetic hour than the classic report-on-the-day somewhere near the kettle late at night!

Jackie Cray also stresses the important role of prayer in the marriage relationship

> We can only 'do it all' by God's grace. Daily prayer is terribly important to me and as a couple we try to pray together every day and keep in close touch with what we're each doing. My tip is: ensure that you have regular conversations with your husband – not only about practical things, but how you are with God, what he's saying to each of you. It is so strengthening to sense that God is at work with you as a couple as well as individually. I'm certainly looking forward to what he has in store.

I am not sure that every couple finds this prayer together so easy though. Please don't feel you should be the same as Davina and Jackie; the dynamics of each marriage are so varied, with personality, church background, past experiences all likely to affect the ways we relate, especially within such a sensitive area as this one, of shared prayer times. How does this work for you?

The word 'intimacy' tends to refer to the sexual aspect of a marriage relationship. Hopefully this is going well most of the time for most married couples but for some it may be curtailed, temporarily or permanently, for reasons of physical or emotional health, because they are apart from each other – or pregnant! At other times marriages come under such strain that making love just becomes too difficult. And of course all this goes on behind closed doors. People looking on, if they even think about it, are likely to just assume that such a minister and his wife are enjoying a normal sex life when in fact this couldn't be further from the truth. I believe this area of marriage is extremely important. It can become a vulnerable spot where the enemy can attack and we can feel isolated and experience a sense of disappointment and failure.

Alison Atkinson summarised a discussion she arranged for the wives of the ministers in training at the Bible college where her husband was Principal. This homed in strongly on the need to guard against sexual temptation and cherish the marriage relationship.

> Men are particularly prone to sexual temptation, although women are by no means immune to it. So for both partners, be aware of the danger of inappropriate relationships with the opposite sex. Vulnerable women in churches can develop an unhealthy interest in the pastor, who seems (and is) approachable, spiritually mature and willing to listen to their problems. Or it may be that there are fellow workers with whom you spend a lot of time; as you work together you get to know them, share spiritual insights, victories and disappointments – and sometimes the line is crossed.

The best defence is the positive route of maintaining good communication within our marriages – I have come up with three 'S's (am I a preacher or what?)

- *Socially* – this means talking! And in this context, being mutually accountable to each other. Openness is essential. It is good to be seen together as a 'strong team' talking to each other in public and about each other to others (in a good way of course!) so that you are thought of as a couple, not just as two individuals.
- *Spiritually* – being on the same wavelength, sharing in prayer, about our walk with God and what he seems to be saying about the work you're in.
- *and Sexually* – what better way to avoid temptation than to enjoy great love-making at home? Good social and spiritual communication – this has positive side-effects on our sex life. (If any husbands need an incentive to pray more with their wives, show them this sentence!)

It's great to have space in our lives as a couple but that may prove harder to come by when there are children around too, in need of attention and entertainment. One advantage of being a church leader, however, is that weekdays are sometimes quite flexible. Many dads are able to take and collect their children to and from school and be there at breakfast and teatime when other men are travelling or still at work. It is a case of swings and roundabouts I suppose; weekends and evenings may be busy but other timeslots can open up. A husband may be out of the house and in church from 6 till 11 several nights a week but perhaps you could enjoy the occasional extended intimate lunchtime, enjoying peace and privacy while the kids are safely out of the way at school. On other less romantic occasions it might be companionable just to be in the garden (so long as it isn't overlooked from the church car park!) or even do some of those necessary chores together.

One of the complications of being married to the leader of your church is that your pastor – whose preaching you hear week in, week out and the person you would normally expect to go to for counselling – is actually your husband. So if you have marriage complications who can you share them with? Someone advised me years ago to pray for God to show me two people I could go to if things got really tough; one, a close girlfriend who would listen, understand, pray and love me whatever I said, and a 'pastor' who would talk straight to me with spiritual authority and wisdom. I discussed this with Lyndon and we agreed who these people could be. He then gave me freedom to say whatever I needed to at any time to either of them. There have been three occasions in our marriage when this has been an absolute lifeline. I am so grateful for God's help and for the trust and love of those special friends.

Sometimes people choose to get a message to the minister via his wife. That might be as simple as 'the prayer meeting is at five o'clock this Tuesday instead of six', or something more devious. One experienced vicar's wife gives this advice

> We found it easy to talk shop at meals and at every other odd minute. We started having what we called an ISM every week – an Informal Staff Meeting – which was a great help. We could talk together for an hour or so over issues and avoid 'chatting church' non-stop.
>
> It is hard to face criticism of one's husband. It took me a while to learn to refuse to pass on criticisms and comments to Bill. I was not going to be a middle man – even though he wasn't perfect!

## When things go wrong

Christian marriages are not immune to problems and stresses – and that includes church leaders. Sadly a number of ministry marriages end each year – in Chapter 10, two women share their experiences of husbands leaving them as a result of an affair.

The following is the personal account of a minister's wife who struggled herself, with becoming attracted to another man. She is determined to restore her marriage, whatever that takes. I suspect a similar story could be told by other women if only they felt there was a 'safe place' to share it. The writer was courageous and desperate enough to find the support she needed. I hope that reading of her experience may encourage anyone who is going through something similar to do the same.

> It had been a tough year for us both in the church and our personal lives. It felt like things were spiralling out of control and we were both pretty exhausted. My husband had become very pessimistic about the future and was suffering from mild depression and it felt that I was the one who had to keep going and hold everything together. Everyone seemed to dump on me. I didn't mind it with the kids – that's motherhood for you isn't it! – but after a while it just became too much. The church treated me as 'the pastor' in my husband's absence, and he leant on me more and more. I really wanted someone to talk to about the way things really were, about what I was feeling.
>
> So that's how the relationship started. He was there. He understood and unloading to him just became a lifeline. We got to the stage of contacting each other each other every day and trying to meet up just for a few minutes here and a few minutes there. Inevitably, I suppose, we ended up in each other's arms. Thank God that's as far as it went but I realised my attraction to this man was

much stronger than anything I felt for my husband. How had this happened to me so easily and what on earth was I going to do? Our entire future hung in the balance; job, home, church life, everything – let alone what would happen to our marriage and the children. There was no question of leaving but my emotions were so strong and I felt so drained. My only human adult source of strength was this man and I recognised we had to put a stop to it. We had tried in our own strength – without success – so decided we each had to admit our situation to someone else. I knew I had to tell my husband too. It felt like being in the middle of a nightmare.

It was actually a huge relief when I plucked up the courage to confess to my friend – she only told me what I already knew; that we needed help and must find it quickly. By now I had brought everything before God and knew he both understood and forgave me. However I still felt a sense of guilt and dread hanging over me. And what of my husband? Needless to say, he was very upset and angry.

Many hours of painful talking followed – question upon question, the inevitable 'why?', counselling sessions and many, many tears. Often it felt like two steps forward and five back but eventually we arrived at a place where we felt we could make our marriage work. It has to work and God will help us. This is what we believe isn't it? With his help and the support of friends and professionals we move forward.

My heart goes out to her and others who may have to cope with all the fall-out on their own, not letting on that anything has gone wrong. Oh for trusted friends who will pray us through these difficulties and give us the strength to do what is right when it seems so hard!

There is another problem that is increasingly experienced in marriages, which bears a huge stigma and causes deep pain. Pornography – especially over the internet where obscene images can sometimes literally be thrown in your face – is regarded by some as seemingly harmless and easily concealed from others, but in reality is devastatingly destructive. And who on earth would one feel able go to for understanding and help? In a recent survey CARE discovered that internet pornography is a growing pastoral concern and is also actually affecting church leaders themselves. A website offering help to them and their families has been set up (www.care.org.uk/anon). As a result, a group of women has started up to create a 'safe place' to encourage and pray for each other about the pain they have experienced because of their spouse's addiction. One of these is Mel (not her real name)

> When I met my husband-to-be, I really thought that he was my knight in shining armour. I needed a knight in shining armour after what I had already been through in my life. Although he was already in his mid-thirties, he had been a Christian since he was seven years old. His parents were missionaries. He had never rebelled or fallen away from the Lord, had a heart and calling for world missions as I did, and best of all, he was still a virgin. Having been abused as a girl, all of this was very important to me. I did not want a husband who had been stained by the world's ideas of sexuality. I earnestly longed for what 'God had intended for good', in a healthy marriage between a husband and wife. After a courtship of fifteen months, we were married in 1992.
>
> After a wonderful honeymoon, we plunged into mission work. It was what we both loved to do. In 1999 we were able to begin full time mission work. By then we were in our second home and had a detached office where my husband was based. My home was a dream come true, but nothing could have prepared me for what was to come.

In September of 2001, on a day that I will never forget, I found out that my husband had a huge secret life. When I confronted him, I expected denial, but instead he admitted it immediately. He was addicted to internet pornography. His viewing of internet porn had begun in our first year of marriage. After ten years with this man, I found myself listening to the life story of someone that I didn't know, a story I had never heard before. While my heart reeled with betrayal, pain and shock, it also grieved for this man as he shared what had been his shameful secret for so many years. He thought that he could control it and that it wasn't hurting anybody, until the internet brought it into his home.

I immediately sought out a friend to talk to ... although this was risky, considering our position as missionaries, I had no choice. For the next year I cried on a daily basis. My relationship with my husband was changed forever, as I finally really knew the man I was married to. We have undergone serious counselling, confession to the president of our mission organisation as well as others, where God has led, and a roller coaster of emotions. We have had three years without internet in the home and now both have support and accountability.

While I would never wish to go through this experience again, and it is far from over, I can see that God has used my husband's sin to refine us both. I can honestly say now that I am grateful for all that has happened and I love my husband more now than I ever did before I really knew him.

In some ways, discovering that your partner regularly accesses porn may be as bad as finding out about a real affair. The following is adapted from an article published by Focus on the Family in the USA on their website.

### *After the Shock*

(When you discover your pastor-husband is ensnared by pornography)
by an anonymous pastor's wife

Little more than eighteen months ago, I stopped by my husband's office at the church to write a quick email while he was gone. My husband had been complaining about how slow his computer was getting, so I decided to take a few minutes to clean up his hard drive. What I discovered needed a 'clean up' of catastrophic size – a problem much worse than just too many files. The real problem was the trails I found to pornographic web sites.

How can I characterize my initial reaction? Somewhere between disbelief and anger. The anger vented itself first as I deleted almost everything on the hard drive in an attempt to punish him and, in a strange way, protect him. If I could find this evidence, so could others. What could this mean to my husband's job, our church, our home and reputation?

A growing number of pastors' wives find themselves with a hard choice. Do I confront my husband and trust him to stop, or go for help and jeopardize everything I hold dear? And, if I seek help, where from? At a time like this, many thoughts and fears pull you in different directions. 'I can't handle this alone.' 'I must protect my husband.' 'I will be so embarrassed.' 'Others will assume I am a bad wife and lover.' 'If he knows I know, he won't dare do it again.'

What I most want to say, is that *you are not alone*. This is a growing problem in the lives of pastors and their families. Other wives are walking this road. Christ grieves over this sin with you, feeling your betrayal by someone you love, understanding how you feel. He too has been betrayed by this servant he loves.

Secondly, you must have help. Walk this road very cautiously and with much prayer, but not alone. Perhaps your best option is to find a godly professional counsellor who works specifically with pastors.

Lastly, don't just seek help for your husband. You are wounded and bleeding. Your heart has been broken and you need to know this 'thing' is not your fault. Get counselling and encouragement for yourself. You may feel all is lost, but keep walking. Trust that your mourning will one day become dancing. With true repentance, restoration can come to your dear one and you. (www.parsonage.org)

## Loyalty and kindness

It may not be as dramatic as the stories above, but every marriage has its hard patches. There have certainly been times in Lyndon's and my relationship when the warm emotions have been frozen out through misunderstanding, disappointment and feelings of neglect. We have a poster on our wall with a text – paraphrased from Proverbs 3:6 – which has become very important to us. Even when loving feelings might seem a little hard to come by, there remains that reality of commitment to one another.

> Never let go of loyalty and kindness.
> Bind them about your neck and write them on your heart.

But marriage needs more than that in the long run. We can all sustain 'dry seasons' but sooner or later passion and deep affection need to be re-established. Pursuing intimacy is a must, even if for some it might require outside help and counselling, as well as continuous, fervent personal prayer that God would help you both.

Killy John says this

> 1 Thessalonians 5:11 says: 'Therefore encourage one another and build each other up'. I strongly believe that in our marriages we need to be encouragers – you can

bury a marriage with a lot of tiny digs. In the last twenty-plus years there have been many times when I have felt down, particularly when the children were very young and John spent a lot of time away from home. At times I felt alone and helpless – but it's so true that you can either let circumstances make you bitter or make you better. I decided that I would be positive and this made a big difference to my outlook and enabled John to fulfil his ministry.

## Some points to consider

The ten most important characteristics contributing to long-term marriages

1. Lifelong commitment
2. Loyalty and faithfulness to your spouse, especially when times are tough
3. Strong moral values you both share
4. Respect for your spouse as your best friend
5. A commitment to sexual fidelity
6. The desire to be good parents
7. Faith in God and a strong faith you want to pass on to your children
8. Wanting to please and support each other
9. Being good companions – spending time together and having fun
10. A willingness to forgive and be forgiven

Would you agree?

(from *Spirituality & Health Magazine* – http://www.spiritualityhealth.com Summer 2000)

# 6. For the Sake of the Children

'Ministry life' gives my son exposure to all kinds of interesting people – much more than if we were in an 'ordinary' job. But his life is much more public and feels a bit looked at! (Anon)

## 'The butterfly'

A man found a cocoon of a butterfly.

One day a small opening appeared.

He sat and watched the butterfly over several hours as it struggled to force its body through that little hole. Then it seemed to stop making any progress. It appeared to have got as far as it could and was unable to push itself any further.

So the man decided to help the butterfly. He took a pair of scissors and very carefully snipped off the end of the cocoon. Now the butterfly could emerge really easily. But he saw it had a swollen body and only small shrivelled wings.

The man continued to watch the butterfly, expecting at any moment to see the wings enlarge and expand to be able to support the body – which would get smaller as time went on.

But neither of these things happened.

In fact the butterfly spent the rest of its brief life crawling around with a swollen body and shrivelled wings. It never flew.

The man in his misplaced kindness and haste did not understand that the restricting cocoon and the struggle required to get through the tiny opening were God's way of forcing fluid from its body into its wings so it would be ready for flight once it achieved its freedom.

Sometimes struggle is exactly what we need in our lives. If God allowed us to go through life without any obstacles it would cripple us. We would never be as strong as we might have been.

We would never be able to fly.

---

I asked for strength and he gave me difficulties to overcome.
I asked for wisdom and he gave me problems to solve.
I asked for prosperity and he gave me brain and brawn to work.
I asked for courage and he gave me danger to overcome.
I asked for love and he gave me troubled people to care for.
I asked for life and he gave me the redeeming cross and triumphant resurrection of the Lord Jesus Christ.
(Author unknown)

I recently shared this story with a group of women and afterwards one of them told me how she used this illustration in her job of training student midwives. 'In delivery, timing is so important,' she said. 'Although on occasions we have to intervene, generally it's best to let nature take its course and the mother to respond to the rhythms in her own body.'

The story of the butterfly has meaning for parents too. There is a Chinese proverb that says: 'We must give our children both roots and wings' and we need daily wisdom to find the right balance between giving our children direction, protection and support and allowing them to help themselves in their spiritual, emotional, intellectual, social and physical development. And bringing them up in the context of church leadership adds further interesting dimensions to this great task.

## Family first

There was broad enthusiastic agreement on this. Time and again women stressed their deepest concern for family life to be enriched. Almost everyone responding to the question: 'What do you pray and wish for most in your marriage and family life?' by saying their chief desire was for children to grow up to love God and live fulfilled lives – as the individuals he had made them to be.

Christine Perkin's comments below are typical of most mothers married to Christian leaders and the way she and Paul have ordered their family life reflects many others

> Our calling must not be worked out at their expense – we must try so hard never allow them to feel resentful of the ministry and read the warning signs:
>
> I remember when the children had all just started full-time school. Up until that time we had always had children's tea at five and then Paul and I would have supper together at any time between seven and eleven at night! We decided that now was the time to have 'grown-up' family time together, and all have supper together at six o'clock. We'd make it special with candles, napkins, pudding... the lot, and really invest serious quality time into it.

But of course, as soon as you make anything a priority – everything and anything will come against it! The phone must have rung a dozen times one particular evening during our 'quality family supper time'. When it went yet again, Max, who must have been about five at the time, jumped up from the table and said, 'I'll answer it.' Paul and I looked admiringly at each other over the table and thought: such a good boy – so sweet and thoughtful...

Max meanwhile picked up the phone and in a theatrical whisper simply said: 'Go away!'

We learnt an important lesson that day!

## Marion White agrees

A day off each week is a biblical command, not an option. 'For six days you shall do your work, but on the seventh day YOU SHALL REST.' That day, for most of us, cannot be a Sunday! Trying to get time together with the family, especially if the spouse has a full-time job as well is very difficult but again very necessary. Space for personal spiritual renewal is also very key for leaders and their spouses. All of this can seem so hard to achieve but it is of vital importance in every area of our lives. I have seen too many burnt-out Christians and those who have been led astray into no-go areas because of extreme weariness. Those of us who are of more mature years should be first in setting the example to younger men and women so that there is not a normal perception of Christian workers who are always tired and worn-out!

Holidays in this job are essential. Short breaks away as a couple are also very helpful. Rob and I have always been totally committed to enjoying decent holidays even when we lived completely by faith and didn't always have the remotest idea of how we could pay for them! In my view holidays, particularly when the family are younger are much more vital than new carpets or furniture. Our children don't always remember that posh new suite but they have lasting memories of special times, playing on the beach or exploring new places, laughing and having fun together as a family.

## 'PK' perks – or problems?

The way family life interacts with ministry obviously changes as the years go by. A portable infant snoozing (or even bellowing) in a carrycot may make little difference – especially if semi-public breast-feeding won't rustle any congregational feather! But once into the toddler stage and with any additional offspring, most mothers find they need to pull back from church life in many ways and spend more time at home. The stability of routine, boring though it may be sometimes, is generally regarded as a better option for small children than semi-permanent 'camping' in church meetings.

Although sometimes it feels as if the church meetings are camping in your home! Patricia Field writes

> Our daughter one day asked me to ask Daddy to come in and kiss her goodnight. Daddy, who was being harangued in the garden by an irate church member, eventually got free and went in much later to her bedroom. He found her sitting up in bed in the dark and saying 'You haven't got time to be my daddy!' Our relationship now is excellent and she has three children of her own.

Many respondents to the questionnaire stressed the benefits they felt their children enjoyed as a result of different people, many of them very interesting, coming back and forth and enriching their lives. The opportunity to meet others is generally seen as a big plus for PKs ('Preachers/Pastors' Kids'). One vicar's wife in a thriving London church says this

> One of the best things about being in ministry is the spin-off for our children. Whilst, like many other children whose parents have busy jobs, there is not always as much leisure time as we'd like, there are so many pluses: being able to eat [a] ... meal together each evening is one of the most important. And another is the opportunities the children get to meet and learn to interact with lots of different people from all walks of life. Our children especially love it when we have visiting speakers to stay with us – they enjoy hearing about their experiences, especially those from overseas, and they really like the gifts they often receive when they leave to go home!

Another mother wrote

> Sometimes my husband's ministry has been a definite bonus for the children as before they started school their dad would often have lunch with them and his evening meetings etc. were after bedtime. Even now he can often attend when they are doing a special assembly or there's an open day.
>
> The downside is when their dad is called away unexpectedly – a person dying or suddenly bereaved. It's difficult to explain why someone else needs their daddy when they were going to do something together.

As they grow older changes may be needed so that the family doesn't feel too exposed, 'in the goldfish bowl'. Jarrod Cooper is very honest about this as he writes about his boyhood

> A pastor's kid, huh? Well don't expect any sympathy. You've got it all. Your dad's a walking concordance, your mum can sing like a canary, no one ever argues in your home, and you: you never feel lonely, lustful, unloved; and you don't have to put up with parents who hate the fact that you're a Christian.

You have the ultimate spiritual environment to live in, of course. Church people are always around your house (what a blast!). Counselling 'cases' ring up at all hours of the day and night, tramps sleep in the spare room, there's always an extra mouth to feed at meal time and you have to go to those exciting church meetings incessantly. Oh yes; there's nothing as great as being a pastor's kid.

In my view there is one thing more important than any other in the Christian life. More important than Bible reading, more important than worship, prayer or ministry; something even more crucial than loving God (now you're worried about me!). It's who you hang out with. You can pray, have a great theology and love God with as much of your heart as you muster, but if you hang out with the wrong people, you'll end up in the wrong place. Very few people are totally unaffected by their friends. Proverbs informs us 'He who walks with the wise grows wise, but a friend of fools suffers harm'. You become like those you hang out with.

We all know people who have loved God, but love him no longer, because they've been friends with the wrong people. Whatever is going on in your life, find quality friends that are going where God wants you to be. I've had lonely times occasionally because there was no one around that I felt was good for me. But I'd rather be lonely and be on fire for God, than be hanging out with people that lead me into grey and compromising lifestyle.

So pastor's kid, yes it's hard, but also a privilege. You have a rich heritage and a special place in God's heart. Break the mould and be yourself. Find friends that will help you get where you want to go as a person and a Christian. Above all, love God, and remember God isn't church; even he gets bored in some of those meetings!

Back on this side of the Atlantic, Vicky Calver reflects on what it means to be in a Christian leader's family, especially one who is well-known. She is deeply appreciative for the way her parents understood and encouraged her but wishes the wider church could be more thoughtful

> If I could plea for anything, it would be that we think seriously [about] how we respond to those who live in the shadows of leadership. I became a Christian at a young age and didn't turn my back on my faith but for me the struggle was feeling that everyone else had expectations of me because of my surname. I wanted to just be me. I remember someone saying, 'It must be wonderful to be the daughter of Clive Calver.' I love my dad dearly but he's my dad. The problem is that if people see the name and not just him, then they tend to see my name and not just me. In this way, as a church, we can end up loving our expectations of each other and not just loving each other.

Both Ruth (Vicky's mum) and Clive were acutely aware of this pitfall and worked hard to encourage each child's individuality. For them family life was the main priority. All four of their children are now in 'full-time' Christian ministry.

Our own son, Daniel, makes his living as a professional magician. (God is always so full of surprises when it comes to our children!) He began to attend a London church where both Lyndon and I are well-known and opted to use his professional name: Daniel Alexander. After a while the leadership discovered his gifts, invited him to share in ministry opportunities and even sent him off to evangelistic events to do magic! Only then (his dad was due to come and preach) did he let it be known that he is a Bowring, through and through. By then he had become accepted and appreciated for who *he* is, not because of who we are.

In the local church the fame of being the vicar's daughter or son may well bring its pressures. Some prefer to worship in a different church and although it might appear awkward this may well be in everyone's best interests even if it is only for a while. The most important thing is for our children to grow up to follow Christ and whatever that takes, let's go for it.

## Just a normal family

Of all the many roles and amazing juggling acts I have seen women married to Christian leaders perform, the one that we invariably prioritise, if we have children, is motherhood. Many feel the need to make up for times when their husband is busy, especially in the evenings, and want to concentrate on being at home to make it a secure and loving place for the family. There are very many advantages for children to be brought up in a church leader's home but it isn't always easy – especially on Sundays! The following was written by Sarah Potter; it may ring bells with you!

> Why is it that Sunday morning always starts so early, or rather Saturday night finishes so late? You would imagine that being a minister's family, we would recognise the need for a good night's sleep before the exploits of Sunday, but frequently somewhere around suppertime, there is that plaintive cry of, 'You remember me telling you about the children's talk tomorrow?' 'Er, vaguely,' I reply, my concentration being diverted by a minor skirmish in the kitchen as one child has sat in another's place, and the other can't find her favourite brown spoon. 'Tell me about it later.'
>
> Later becomes much later as bedtime take forever and I am quizzed on how old God is, if Jesus liked McDonalds

and the likelihood of the cat going to heaven. Why is it that you can never find a minister when you need one? 'Particularly urgent pastoral phone calls' I'm told – chatting about football more like.

Anyway, back to the task in hand, 'I just need you to write a few things on a flip chart, and draw a pie chart on acetate.' It's not that my writing is particularly neat or my drawing particularly good, quite the reverse in fact, but it is ever so slightly better than my husband's and that means it is my job. I spend the first half hour carefully measuring lines and practising fitting the words on. I'm sure there must be specialised drawing equipment that would speed the process up (either that or an assertiveness course, 'No darling, I think you should do it, anyway I have got some particularly urgent pastoral calls to make too.') I finally get page two done, having carefully avoided ink splodges and then the cat walks across it leaving muddy footprints – the question of cats and heaven may be answered sooner than we think!

By this point I've decided that as long as it's legible, I'll be happy; I just want my bed – why oh why did he not ask me sooner?

I keep saying I'm going to write to one of the theological colleges, suggesting a suitable course for minister's wives. One module would be called, 'Art and flip chart design for the creatively-challenged and sleep-deprived'.

I have to say that I do find Sundays rather stressful. Children to dress in clothes that vaguely go together, husbands to advise ('Do you think this tie goes with this shirt? Oh! The shirt has lost a button and my trouser pocket has a hole in it!'), breakfast to organise ('But I don't like cornflakes anymore, they were my favourite yesterday, that's ages ago, Mummy!') and, due to an unfortunate accident, now bedding to wash. I'm sure numbers of people would disapprove of me doing the washing on a Sunday, but the resulting chaos on a Monday would leave the manse looking even more like a Chinese laundry. (Mental note: ask colleges to provide a course entitled, 'Basic grooming and survival skills for men'.)

After a scramble to find matching shoes, lost keys and a tense discussion on why they can't take a rugby ball to church, we embark on that activity known as loading the car: who is going to sit where (preferred places change hourly); has Daddy got everything he needs and why is the car door making that funny noise? The children engage us in discussion on the way there about the fantastic ages reached by some Old Testament characters, and one of them, dutifully reading her way through Genesis asks, 'What does circumcision mean, Daddy?' 'Ask your Sunday school teacher,' he replies.

And it's still only a quarter to ten!

As children get older, more and more time can be taken up with homework and other activities. In our marriage 'managing' the children has been mainly my department and I have thoroughly appreciated the freedom to be a stay-at-home mother. But child-rearing has stressful moments for everyone and when Dad's a vicar there may be added pressures. Fiona Perry wrote this article for Living with Leadership's newsletter *REAL* in 2003

The title of this parenting course title often resonates with me: 'Help, I'm the Parent!' Andy and I have three children, two teenagers and one still a 'tweenie' – who actually fits the stereo-typical category of teenager the most! They are lively, gorgeous and delightful… and frequently cause me to refine and fine-tune my parenting skills!

My husband is vicar of a church in Poole. We love the ministry here but now and again the pressures of Andy's work demand a huge amount of his time and energy. Of course he is deeply involved and interested in our children, but I sometimes feel a bit on my own when it comes to helping them with coursework and homework, deciding which 'out of school' activities will bring out their best, and even how to nurture and release them in their own spiritual walk. It can almost feel we're in a tug-of-war, with me pulling Andy in one direction and the church, albeit unintentionally, in the other.

Perhaps you've had similar experiences. We have reflected a lot about this issue and discussed how best to cope with these feelings.

- Sometimes an added pressure is that we are juggling too much ourselves – children, work, church involvement… and maybe need to stand back and ask if we're doing more than the Lord asks of us.
- It's a comfort to recognize that our husbands can be particularly busy just for a season. Then, let's claim God's promise to *'supply all our needs according to his riches in glory'* and support them, willingly releasing them to lead the church through especially demanding times and rely on the Lord for extra love and strength.
- Maybe there are important underlying issues. Has the rhythm and pace of life actually become unsustainable and potentially damaging for us as individuals, in our marriage and for our children? If so, together or perhaps even with the help of a trusted friend, we need to bring this imbalance and feeling of being on our own out in the open; to talk, pray and find a way forward. Expressing our concerns, aspirations and frustrations; accepting one another with forgiveness and love will lead to rediscovering the equilibrium that's needed.

We're in all of this together and in reality the course should be called 'Help we're *both* the Parents!'

Going back to the issue of expectations, many ministers' wives with children feel the pressure to help in the crèche or Sunday school. When Lyndon and I were at Kensington Temple I was a primary school teacher. Certain members of the church felt that this automatically qualified me to help with the children on Sunday mornings. The reality was that I welcomed a break from my profession at the weekend. Far more interesting and fruitful to stay in the service!

One respondent wrote

> I recently resigned from the Sunday School because I felt I was missing out on receiving teaching in church. I felt guilty about this, more so because I am the vicar's wife but being a single parent on a Sunday morning with three young children to look after is no picnic. And now, when they leave for their classes I am so grateful to sit back and listen to the sermon.
>
> It may just be my perception but I do feel that people are watching my children's behaviour in church and that puts pressure on me (and perhaps them). I am probably stricter than if I were just a normal member of the congregation. On the positive side, I think they're made more of a fuss of because they're the vicar's children.

Some women report that people in their churches have a strange expectation that the minister's children will be perfectly behaved. I once found a cartoon of a scandalised crèche volunteer regarding a wailing infant squirming in his stinking nappy. 'I am surprised! This is the *vicar's* son!' she says, disapprovingly. Our children are likely to be like anyone else's although we never stop praying that they will find a living relationship with God and grow up to love and serve him.

Finding out that we are normal should make us more real to people so they can relate to the fact that we face the same struggles as they do. Christine Freeland says

> Children can be our greatest asset – especially in the difficult periods of their upbringing. The whole village watched once as their new minister and his wife were enthusiastically greeted by an eighteen-year-old apparition – with torn jeans, laceless boots, dyed Mohican hair, ironmongery dripping from his ears as he walked from the station through the Fête on the Green. This proved to be an invaluable starting point for relationships of trust with many a distraught parent!
>
> Other Christians and other churches have played a crucial role in the nurture of our two sons for which we are eternally grateful. Each has gone through a period of disillusionment with the church but nothing has removed the foundations laid and the knowledge that we have been loved and supported as a family throughout our ministry.

God entrusts some of us with sons and daughters who choose to follow really difficult paths, perhaps to date rejecting the church and all Christianity stands for. In some cases this is for good reason. I know of ministry families who have been poorly treated by their church fellowships and have suffered rejection, slander, unfair accusations and worse. Children pick these things up and can be deeply hurt and disillusioned at such treatment of their parents by the very people for whom they pour out their lives.

One person wrote this

> Loyalty to kids is a high priority for us. I did not share their failings with the church. People could know mine – but not theirs. One day one of our teenage boys had a drinking session with his friends after the exams. They were really drunk and I had to get them out of the house without the PCC meeting downstairs knowing. I did not see this as protecting my pride but protecting them.

Praying for our prodigals is something we *can* do; and that our local churches will become increasingly prodigal-friendly – especially to the wounded and disillusioned children of some church leaders, to their grief and sorrow.

Killy John feels very deeply for young people like this and strongly believes in the part prayer has to play

> Isaiah 54:13 'All your children will be taught by the LORD and great will be your children's peace.' In his book, *Bringing Back the Prodigals* (Hodder and Stoughton, 2003), Rob Parsons wrote this, which I found very helpful: 'We cannot bring up godly children, it is not our responsibility – it is too heavy – we are called instead to live godly lives.' He then goes on to say, 'I believe that prayer is our only hope.'
>
> My grandmother used to question the statement 'we can only pray,' and say, 'why do we make it sound like a last resort, instead of a first point of contact?' Coming from a family heritage of Christian leaders, I have heard many wonderful stories and can certainly say prayer works. Obviously as parents we will pray but it helps if others pray too. Whatever our opinions of infant baptism, dedication or thanksgiving, we can slot in godparents, choose prayerfully and wisely and get them to commit to praying for the child. If they fall by the wayside, adopt new ones! On the day before our wedding, John and I went to collect my grandparents from the station. With tears in their eyes they said, 'All the years we have prayed God would send you a Christian man and look! He has given you an evangelist.'

## Special children

All children are special, of course, and every one of them has areas in their lives requiring specific help.

However some of our children have particular needs which bring their own challenges and grace-blessings into our lives. The survey revealed that 15 per cent of the families included children with special needs – and sometimes there were more than one in the home. This high figure indicates the added pressures many leaders are under as they deal with sometimes difficult situations alongside church life. Fifteen children were affected by dyslexia and almost twenty with autistic, Asperger's and other associated disorders.

The following is a selection of some specific problems mentioned

> Our youngest has severe epilepsy. He had brain surgery at two and is physically and emotionally delayed.
>
> The two eldest are fostered and have emotional and behavioural needs.
>
> The older has special needs and is in a residential school, the younger one is very difficult.

Nobody can know what another's situation is really like. There are both great joys and deep heartache in parenting anyway, and this is also so for those with a child with special needs. There are many stories to tell, each different and in the main testifying to God's goodness in the midst of everything. This is what happened with our daughter, born in 1984

> The pregnancy had given rise to some concern, but the birth was uneventful. But when she was six weeks old we were told our baby had an unusual syndrome with a long list of possible symptoms that threatened to affect her very seriously. Her sight was severely impaired, and in particular, she had no macula in either eye. 'She is as good as blind,' they told us sadly, and sent us home, shell-shocked at this news.

At the time Lyndon and I were in the pastoral ministry at Kensington Temple and, as you can imagine, we were surrounded by loving Christians who assured us of their prayers and offered practical help too – like the saintly lady who did my ironing for several weeks. Being a Pentecostal church, there was a strong belief in God's power and willingness to heal and of course we agreed that this was wholly possible and were grateful for the faith and fervour of many in the congregation. However, after a while I found all this attention hard to cope with. While most people in the church were wonderfully sensitive and caring there were some who wanted to physically lay hands on our very unsettled and disorientated baby and others exhorting us to pray ever harder and not give the devil any foothold. I came to the point where I dreaded going to church; Lyndon and I needed room to adjust and time to grieve over this visual disability – and the other possible complications we feared could blight her life.

We were exhausted from the demands not only of our new baby but also her strong-willed eighteen-month-old brother. He already felt displaced and was now in danger of neglect as I dealt with all the hospital visits and doctors' appointments necessary (almost one hundred in her first year). Thankfully the initial diagnosis proved to be overly pessimistic and she was doing well but there were still considerable problems to face and Lyndon and I sometimes felt overwhelmed. It was at a leaders' conference that Roger and Faith Forster spoke to us firmly. 'Stop praying all the time for her to be healed,' Roger ordered us, to our surprise. 'That's the body of Christ's job and we will ask our church to fast and pray for her. God wants you to love your precious child exactly the way she is, unconditionally. You can't do that if you are desperately interceding for her to be different.' These were such wise words; setting us free to pour our love into her life, to build her up and find positive ways to help her in the shadow world she inhabited physically.

> Many Christians prayed and God did touch her eyes. A few months later I noticed a considerable improvement in her visual awareness and at our next appointment at London's famous Moorfields Eye Hospital doctors acknowledged there had actually been a miracle – they agreed on this word. The macula in each eye had grown and when examined 'looked immature and still developing, as if these were the eyes of an unborn child.' From seeing little more than light and dark our baby began to take notice of toys and look around at her surroundings. Her sight gradually improved – although she is still not completely healed and today is registered as partially sighted. There were many challenges for her to overcome as she grew up and it was not always easy.
>
> Currently she is at university, training in Occupational Therapy and she adores travelling abroad 'having adventures' as often as she can find the money and the time. One of her desires is to return to Africa and help children with HIV/AIDS in a Christian centre there. Lyndon and I are overwhelmed by God's grace in her life and thankful for everything she has taught us and all she means to us.

Other parents have far greater tests to contend with, having to watch over their children through sickness, disability, mental illness and the fall-out from unwise choices and unfavorable friends. Others grieve because they have never been able to have a baby, or a child has died.

Whether our children are young or have grown to adults they still have such a big part of our hearts. The Bible says

> Children are a gift from the LORD; they are a reward from him.
> (Ps. 127:3, NLT)

Emma, the daughter of the Salvation Army's founder General Booth, said this about her mother Catherine. What a tribute!

> She was the light of our lives, the inspiration of our childhood, the ideal of our ambitions, the repository of our confidence, the guardian angel of our souls and the beacon of our lives as we sailed earth's sea towards the same blissful harbour in which she dropped anchor forever.

## Some points to consider

1. Are we aware of how our children feel and think about their situation? How can we give them opportunity and space to express this?
2. How can we practically work out the priorities of family life in the context of ministry demands and responsibilities?
3. What specific prayers of thanksgiving and requests are we making on behalf of our children? How has God answered in the past?

# 7. Called, Contented – Or Cornered?

I trained for ordination as a church minister myself and we married just before I finished at college. He is the vicar and I'm the part-time associate, a full time mother and up until recently working part time as chaplain in a local secure training centre. (Anon)

## 'The cracked pot'

A water bearer in India had two large pots, each hung on each end of a pole which he carried across his neck. One of the pots had a crack in it, and while the other pot was perfect and always delivered a full portion of water at the end of the long walk from the stream to the master's house, the cracked pot arrived only half full. For a full two years this went on daily, with the bearer delivering only one and a half pots full of water in his master's house. Of course, the perfect pot was proud of its accomplishments. But the poor cracked pot was ashamed of its own imperfections, and miserable that it was able to accomplish only half of what it had been made to do.

After two years of what it perceived to be a bitter failure, the pot spoke to the water bearer one day by the stream. 'I am ashamed of myself, and I want to apologize to you.' 'Why?' asked the bearer. 'What are you ashamed of?' 'I have been able, for these past two years, to deliver only half my load because this crack in my side causes water to leak out all the way back to your master's house. Because of my flaws, you have to do all of this work and you don't get full value for your efforts,' the pot said.

The water bearer felt sorry for the old cracked pot and in his compassion he said, 'As we return to the master's house I want you to notice the beautiful flowers along the path.'

Indeed, as they went up the hill, the old cracked pot took notice of the sun warming the beautiful wild flowers on the side of the path, and this cheered it some. But at the end of the trail, it still felt bad because it had leaked out half its load, and so again it apologized to the bearer for its failure.

The bearer said to the pot, 'Did you notice that there were flowers only on your side of the path but not on the other pot's side? That's because I have always known about your flaw, and I took advantage of it. I planted flower seeds on your side of the path, and every day while we walk back from the stream, you've watered them. For two years I have been able to pick these beautiful flowers to decorate my master's table. Without you being just the way you are, he would not have this beauty to grace his house.'

Each of us has our own unique flaws. We're all cracked pots. But if we will allow it, the Lord will use those same imperfections to bring about good. In God's great economy, nothing goes to waste.

(The Cracked Pot:
See http://www.eakles.com.81flawpage.htm)

2 Timothy 2:21 says: 'If you keep yourself pure, you will be a special utensil for honorable use. Your life will be clean, and you will be ready for the Master to use you for every good work.' (NLT) Whatever the shape,

positioning and extent of the cracks in our lives, it is our heart attitude to the Lord that matters; whether we are obedient and willing for him to use us as he pleases. How is he calling us?

## Called by name

The musician Sir Bob Geldof's four daughters have intriguing names: Fifi Trixibelle, Peaches Honeyblossom, Pixie, and Heavenly Hiraani Tiger Lily! Not many of us have risen to the occasion with quite such panache but all the same – whether or not they grow up to be grateful for it, we the parents get to decide what our children are to be called.

In the Bible names carry significance and meaning and this is also true today, especially in many Asian and African cultures. I was thrilled therefore to discover at an early age that my own name, Celia, comes from the Latin word for sky – or heaven maybe! Imagine my disappointment when my mother told me the reason she chose it was because she really liked the actress Celia Johnson. But more importantly, I can look forward in anticipation to discovering what *new* name God has for me, in heaven.

> And I will give to each one a white stone, and on the stone will be engraved a new name that no one knows except the one who receives it. (Rev. 2:17, NLT)

One of the distinctives of Christian faith is that God is the initiator. He calls us by name individually, and yet we have the free will to choose his ways or not. Before we were ever interested in him, he called us to be saved and made new in Christ. When God speaks to us – as he does each day – how do we answer? Sometimes, like our own children, do we avoid responding for some reason? Adam hid because he felt guilty, Gideon because he was afraid and Jonah because he was angry about what God had told him to do. But God doesn't give up that easily and he understands our humanity. The calling of God is a serious issue, both for our individual destiny and how others will be affected by our response. Finding out the where, when, how and what of our lives is crucial even though the details and unexpected twists and turns are not yet visible to us.

> For we are God's workmanship, created in Christ Jesus to do good works, which God prepared in advance for us to do. (Eph. 2:10, NIV)

He calls us to many things: a task, a way of life, a person, family, church, community – at different times and in various ways, to serve him. And the discovery may not always be a delight in the first place, or as the journey continues through difficult places, and we find ourselves wondering…

## Called to the ministry?

Life often turns out differently from how we imagined. How many of us, in our youth, confidently set out along a certain path of career, relationship or lifestyle only to find it petering out or radically changing in direction as time passed? As we look back, perhaps many of our original dreams and expectations have come to pass but other plans, once so definite, have changed or been abandoned altogether. I wonder if, like me, you sometimes reflect on the past and wonder how on earth you got from where you started from to where you are today.

Here's Helen Clarke

> 'I will never marry a minister!' said I at fifteen, struggling with aspects of living in a rectory in the middle of Ireland, an MK (Minister's Kid). How God smiles at us and I can smile with him as I think back over the thirty years Ken and I have been in the ministry together, mostly in the Province but now back in the South of Ireland. We've shared mountains of joy and many valleys of heartache, times of fulfilment and those of utter exhaustion. At times I have wrestled with role identity in living with leadership. Working in partnership with a husband in ministry means many different things to different people, both inside and outside the local church. But from what I've seen, both as a MK and a MW (Minister's Wife) – now married to a bishop – there are few people and places where it is safe to take the risk of being too open and vulnerable. Meeting together with others in similar circumstances through our Living with Leadership groups has great potential for creating such opportunities.

I know many women who like Helen vowed never to marry a vicar but found God had other plans. Certainly if anyone had said to me at sixteen years old that within five years I would be married to a minister of religion, I would have responded with horrified incredulity at such a thought. I grew up as a fairly typical Sixties teenager in a loving secure family and only ever attended church on very odd occasions – for Brownie Church Parades and occasionally at Easter and Christmas. When the time came to select a college to train as a primary teacher, I purposely chose one of the very few with no church affiliation, knowing for sure I wanted nothing to do with religion. That first day, as I breathlessly arrived on my bike eager to embark on this new chapter, my mind was buzzing with ideas and questions about the meaning of existence in general, and mine in particular. Within an hour I was sitting over coffee with a group of Christian students who God would use to change my future forever as they lovingly listened to my arguments and prayed for me. They welcomed me into their rooms, shared their food and their thoughts and so within a term and a half I became convinced that Jesus was real and that I could not live without him. On Valentine's Day, in an evangelistic service at Kensington Temple, I became a Christian.

In the years since, God (well, I hope it was always him) has called me to do all kinds of things, some scary, some boring, some creative and much of it very hard work. Most of the time I have felt seriously lacking in confidence and wished there was more encouragement around for people like me as I have tried to get to grips with what God wanted.

One set of questions in our survey looked at this whole issue of 'calling'. The responses were interesting. One of my favourite comments was, 'I told my boyfriend that we were going to work for God, and so we did'. On the other end of the scale this woman said, 'No. I cannot honestly say that I have ever felt called to ministry and would rather not be, but from the start I have actively supported my husband.' One spoke of 'being called as an individual, to help others and come alongside those hurting'. Another: 'I had prayed for a mature Christian husband. I suppose falling in love with him was the beginning of my calling. Before becoming a Christian I had always had a pastoral role with my friends.'

There is a strong feeling among many women I have met, and who took part in the survey, that their calling is not to 'be a minister's wife' so much as to be themselves and do what God has called them to. For example one person who had been in the situation for more than twenty-five years wrote

> We have always tried to keep to the policy that I would only take on what I would have done in the church anyway – not because I was 'the rector's wife'. We support one another in our own careers – him being a 'teacher's husband' is equally important.

## What does it mean?

Christine Freeland had a strong sense of God calling her into ministry but sometimes found it difficult to work out what it meant practically.

> I believe I was called to partnership in the ministry, but I have often felt on a see-saw or roller coaster in terms of confidence. On the one hand there is an overwhelming sense of love and trust and approval from the Lord and his people (often undeserved) and on the other a desperate feeling of inadequacy, even worthlessness (often irrational). 'Just who do you think you are?' and 'What good do you really think you are doing?' 'Where do you belong in this community?' etc. are all challenges I hear from our accuser – the devil whispering to my heart. This is when I feel cornered.

While Alison Atkinson's husband was Principal of Regents Bible College she brought together the students' spouses to consider some of the issues facing them as they prepared for pastoral ministry within the Elim

Movement. She put together six questions which they found useful to talk through together

1. How do you know that your husband is called to be a pastor?
2. How involved were you in his decision to go into ministry?
3. Do you have a sense of 'calling' on your own life?
4. How does this fit into your husband's call?
5. What do you think other people's expectations of you will be?
6. To what extent is it right to conform to others' expectations?

This is how she summarised their discussions around each question

1. The call to ministry comes in various forms. As wives we may not have been directly involved in our husband's call, but surely we must, at some stage be completely behind (or preferably beside) them, convinced that *they* are called, and doing all we can to help them to fulfil their vision from God.
2. For some, calling comes after marriage when it is particularly important for husband and wife to be in agreement. Others marry in the full knowledge that God has called them into ministry, so at least they should be going into it with their eyes open! Either way unity is important; it is hard to be a pastor's wife who resents her husband's ministry. If, deep down, you know that you are called by God (together) it will be harder for negativity to gain a foothold in your life.
3. This can be a problem for wives whose husbands study at Bible college while they do the supporting full-time job, look after the children, the home and all

the other essentials. Such women sometimes feel at a disadvantage but they shouldn't. *We* can get before God and find out what he wants us to do, asking to be made aware of the gifts we have and seeking God for more. To begin with we are called to be the best wife our husband could have – he will need our support, friendship, prayer backing and love. Some of us will have a 'public' role as well but it's important to be sure this is given by God and we can recognise what *he* wants to accomplish through us.

4. Our various roles need to dovetail. We are 'one flesh' and neither of us can just storm ahead with what we feel is a calling from God without reference to our other half. Very often husbands and wives complement each other in ministry – maybe one preaches challenging sermons and the other quietly encourages individuals. One a good organiser and the other a visionary.

5. Rest assured, they will have some! We probably won't measure up to everyone's expectations but forewarned is forearmed – it's God's expectations that are important.

6. Here is the nub of the matter. Do we get on exclusively with what we know is 'our calling' and refuse to do anything else (and thereby offend people) or do we smile graciously and do what is expected of us? Of course, the answer is somewhere between the two. There is a place for doing things because they need to be done, even if we don't feel it is 'our ministry'. That is part of being a servant of God; he supplies the gifts we need for the occasion and often surprises us by helping us to enjoy it. On the other hand we need to avoid being squeezed into a mould. I designed a questionnaire for pastors' wives last year. The most prevalent piece of advice they gave was 'Be yourself!'

Interestingly the same is true of our survey.

## Called to be what?

Generally it seems to me that the position of the minister's wife is not taken sufficiently seriously either at the training stage or when the time comes to take a job. The church generally doesn't employ her but sometimes has the unspoken expectation that she will play her part – whether that's engaging in some specific activity like running the mums and toddlers, pastoring the ladies or forever organising refreshments. When we asked people responding in our survey to tick all the various activities in which they were involved as a leader or part of a team, 423 individuals replied as follows (approximately)

| | |
|---|---|
| Hospitality | 330 |
| Children's work | 204 |
| Women's ministries | 204 |
| Visiting | 164 |
| Speaking | 158 |
| Administration | 148 |
| Youth ministries | 101 |

Being in the ministry isn't quite the same as any other occupation. Other jobs may be more demanding: for example serving in the Armed Forces, or running a business perhaps. Politicians hardly have it easy either. But church ministry carries spiritual responsibility on top of all the other aspects of working in a church and the wife will be drawn into that whether she likes it or not.

Working out our calling as 'the wife' when no one else is particularly interested is not easy. This writer however did receive some helpful input

> I have struggled with a lack of a real sense of calling but more recently someone prophesied over me about hospitality and leadership. I could understand the hospitality as I *love* cooking but couldn't see the leadership ever happening. Over the last eighteen months however I have started leading services and have had some very positive feedback. I'm exploring setting up a women's group now and have a greater sense of 'call' than just responding to people's needs. This obviously fits in with my husband very well! I would love to develop working alongside him more in the future but am unsure how to do it.

Wendy was brought up in a strong, loving Christian family. She had surrendered her life to Christ at a tender age and was confident that there was a great future ahead for her. As she grew up, many missionaries and visiting ministers stayed in her parents' home and Wendy loved listening to the enthralling stories they shared. Sometimes she was asked 'What has God called you to?' but right into her late teens she had to admit that she'd never received the burning message, no unmistakable burden for that special place somewhere in the world for which she was divinely destined. And then one Sunday morning Wendy received 'her call'. Listening to the enthusiastic young preacher, she suddenly knew, without a shadow of doubt, what God had in mind: that 'your calling is to Terry Virgo' and now, more than three decades on, she is no less sure than she was then. Wendy Virgo is an author, a well-known speaker, mentor and encourager to thousands of women, but she would say her most important ministry has been to support her husband and to raise their four sons.

## Preparing for ministry

I have met many women who married a husband happily ensconced in whatever job he had chosen only to find later that God was calling him into full-time ministry. I think it is very important for the church to have a good number of clergy who have lived in the 'real world' and know what it is like to work amongst non-Christians – having to be an effective witness for Christ in an often alien environment. But for the wives, this turn of events is sometimes rather a shock. Living with Leadership regularly visited colleges to encourage student spouses, many of whom were 'mature', as they prepared to take on the role of the curate's or minister's wife. Some were enthusiastic and others apprehensive. All of them greatly valued the friendships they made in those training years which often were to continue for years to come. They also appreciated sharing with those of us who were already 'in the saddle' and able to allay their fears, encouraging them to step out with confidence and faith for the future.

Christine Perkin was particularly involved in coming alongside these student spouses. She writes

> Many will recall the years at Theological or Bible college with mixed emotions: excitement of starting something fresh, sadness of leaving what was safe and familiar, stimulation from being in a learning environment, apprehension about what (and where) may be ahead, and anxieties over children, finances and our abilities.
>
> This training period can be a testing time; my memories certainly all came flooding back when we visited several colleges last year to bring vision and encouragement … [to] the wives of students preparing for ministry. Life at college can have its vulnerable moments and we should encourage one another – yes, being realistic about the

pressures and the expectations, but reminding each other that 'He who called us is faithful' and that there is fulfilment and joy too.

Judy is married to Dr Nigel Wright, Principal of Spurgeons College. She is a trained counsellor and also takes a particular interest in their students' spouses – both men and women – organising regular activities for them. Students preparing for the Baptist ministry are usually based in churches over a far flung area throughout their training so it is much more difficult for the wives to meet together because mostly they live a long way apart.

Theological college is a strange place to be; or to be more precise, the time spent there is strange, an in-between time – at least it can seem that way for the spouses of those training for ministry. For some it is a period of major upheaval, perhaps changing job, moving house and being in a different church. For all there is a period of adjustment – to changes in their present lives and lifestyles and to facing an unknown future.

And what will the future hold? Gone, we hope, is the automatic stereotypical image of a minister's wife, to be replaced by something more commensurate with our gifts and our passion to serve God. But how can we prepare for this? Colleges can offer opportunities to spouses for training in various skills (counselling, evangelism, leading worship etc.), but a focus on *relationships* will provide both present support and equipping for the future.

- *Building strong supportive friendships.*
  Good friendships made outside of our church situations (either at college or in the small groups encouraged by LWL and other organisations) will be supportive throughout our ministry lives.

- *Learning to accept ourselves.*
  We dream of what we can achieve for the Lord – or maybe we fear we will fail to live up to expectations – our own as well as those of other people. The *Lord* will work with our unique combination of gifts, personality and circumstances to fulfil *his* mission in our lives.
- *Discovering more of the love of Christ for us.*
  This continuing journey is the underpinning for all our relationships and the key to accepting ourselves. To explore the depth of his love for us is a lifelong occupation and delight as we seek to serve him in whatever way he calls us.

## Changing roles – beyond the local church

While most Christian leaders spend their working lives in a local church context many others branch out into different ministries 'parachurch'. This happened to Lyndon and me after ten years at Kensington Temple when it became gradually clear that we should move, to work with CARE; an organisation that grew out of the Nationwide Festival of Light rally in Trafalgar Square back in 1971. This event had been held to signal the rising concern of churches from all denominations over the decline in Christian standards and values in public life in the aftermath of the permissive sixties. By 1980 the situation had only worsened and Lyndon and Charlie Colchester were asked to take on the joint leadership of the renamed 'CARE' to try to mobilise the church and make a Christian difference in Parliament and other places of influence in the nation; particularly on issues such as abortion, euthanasia and obscenity.

At that time, although we were struggling to come to terms with being told we were extremely unlikely ever to have a baby of our own, I was really finding my feet as a pastor's wife, enjoying the opportunity to develop my gifts, and be available to encourage and help the people in the church. I had left teaching so as to be freer so this turn of events took me by surprise and I vividly remember talking to the Lord as I walked home one day. 'What's all this fuss about abortion? Surely the main thing is to work in the church. We're happy there. Lyndon's good at preaching, he's a great pastor. What's going on here? Why does he want to leave? So tell me, how do *you* feel about abortion? Is it *that* important to you?'

I thought no more of it until some months later we were together on the platform of the Methodist Central Hall, Westminster at an event to commemorate the passing of the 1967 Abortion Act. We all stood in silence as thousands of white paper petals gently cascaded with a whispering sound from the roof. Without warning I felt a terrible tearing in my heart and began to weep bitterly for these precious lost lives and sensed God saying 'This is a tiny fraction of what I feel. It's as much as you can bear.' I have worked alongside Lyndon with all my heart in the ministry of CARE ever since.

Being in parachurch ministry is very different. One issue is how you fit in to a local church; it is not always easy. Moving away from a local church role may mean you are still part of the denomination but no longer attached to a particular fellowship. I have met many women married to bishops or their non-Anglican equivalent who have had to really seek God to reassess what they should be doing and where they can find a spiritual home, especially for the family.

Jackie Cray worked for many years with Church Pastoral Aid Society during which time she wrote two books about ministry to children in the church. Married to Graham, she experienced years of parish ministry before they moved on to the very different world of the theological college where Graham was appointed Principal. While there Jackie involved herself with the students (and their spouses). Graham then became Bishop of Maidstone. Jackie is now ordained herself and has always enjoyed the variety her life has brought as she has 'lived with leadership' to the full.

> Life changed when Graham was appointed Bishop of Maidstone. On the positive side, there are lots of gospel and ministry opportunities as we travel around different churches – sometimes two or three on a Sunday, plus the mid-week services. But we miss living and ministering within a real community. Previously we had so much prayer and support from both the parish we worked in and at Wycliffe Theological College. You are very much 'on your own' as the bishop and his family.
>
> We live in a very manageable modern five-bedroomed house in a village (that's a totally new experience!) Everybody knows who we are but we don't know them. I *slowly* made contact with our neighbours but if it wasn't for the prayerful and caring network of people that God has given us over the years, it could be very isolating.
>
> Before this, at college, life was very different. I very much enjoyed interacting with the staff, students and their spouses. I had loved being in a parish too (despite the tough times) and wanted to inspire and encourage others at Wycliffe to see that being a leader's wife is a great privilege presenting unique opportunities. It is exciting to see how women respond to this challenge differently, according to their own individual gifts and ministries.

Increasingly couples are finding themselves led into the ministry at a later stage in life. I have lost count of the number of women who have told me with a wry smile; 'Well, when we got married he was a teacher/lawyer/banker/farmer. I never dreamed this would happen!' They now find themselves supporting their husband through a theological college course and face the prospect of becoming a curate's wife, unsure of all the expectations that go along with this role. Some plan to continue in their careers as teachers, nurses, civil servants or whatever. Others sense that this new beginning will involve them heavily as well and are excited/apprehensive (usually both) about their future ministry alongside their husband in whatever form that will take.

> I fought against my husband's call. We explored with many Christian friends and leaders for two-and-a-half years before I had the peace of mind that it was of God and not my husband going through another career change or a mid-life crisis!

Pam Bendor-Samuel has worked in Bible Translation ministry for most of her life. God has used her and blessed her in so many ways and she looks back with gratitude for such a fulfilling half century.

> We have been married 50 years this summer, and John has been a leader from the word 'go' – here in UK and since 1962 in the spread of the SIL and Wycliffe work in Africa. So we have worked under several different sets of circumstances (and in some ways, I feel very out of touch with work here in UK), but I am sure many if not all of the principles of interaction and sharing between husband and wife must be the same. We have been privileged to be partners in the work all that time, each in different fields (I as a translation consultant) – though we have both shared in the training here in UK for many years. Our five grown children and spouses are serving the Lord in various ways, and there have been the joys

and challenges of weaving together ministry and family. I believe the Lord wants a unified 'wholeness' in our lives whether we are washing dishes, writing a letter, speaking to someone, behind a desk or whatever.

Killy John believes

> We will all be different with what we do with our lives and God has a unique plan for each one of us. I love the verse in Jeremiah 29:11, 'For I know the plans I have for you,' says the LORD. 'They are plans for good and not for disaster, to give you a future and a hope.' (NLT)

Finding contentment is so important even when we are not living in our preferred world. Paul 'learned to be content whatever the circumstances. I know what it is to be in need, and I know what it is to have plenty. I have learned the secret of being content in any and every situation, whether well fed or hungry, whether living in plenty or in want. I can do everything through him who gives me strength.' (Phil. 4:11,12, NIV) That's quite something to live up to! We need the discernment to know when we must knuckle down to be content in unfulfilling tasks and when it is right not to agree to do them. I guess that many ministry wives do feel cornered and rather taken for granted and unappreciated for who they really are.

David Crabb, a minister in Rugby, has written with great appreciation about his wife

> Over thirty years ago Sheila became a stabilising influence in a life that was out of control. Somehow, she managed to keep me anchored but has also helped to release the very best parts of me. We have been best friends since the day we first met. The times my poor wife has sat in

the congregation blushing or covering her face with her hands at the outrageous things I have said or done – usually slips of the tongue, or said with tongue in cheek. It does seem at times as though I have stumbled and blundered through life with Sheila following on, picking up the pieces of the trail left behind me.

How many churches, I wonder, do anything at all in terms of honouring their pastor's wife? Most ministers' wives remain nameless, title-less, in the background yet with incredible expectations placed upon them. What a job! Not quite a pastor because she hasn't been ordained or attended Bible college, yet qualified enough to be entrusted with the job of pastoring us. There are few, if any, training courses for ministers' wives (or husbands). They are seldom honoured in the way they should be. Yet they are expected to share the pressures, [and] demands of church leadership as are their families.

The pastor will be supported in the early years through seminars, conferences all designed to enhance his newly formed skills. But what preparation is being done for pastors and their families just to be able to deal with life whilst in the ministry? What does a wife say when visiting the family whose daughter has just been murdered by a church member? What does she say to the drug addict's mother? What does she say to the woman who needs to speak to her about sexual abuses that have happened, perhaps still happen? What training is being offered to our wives?

Sheila Crabb is a great example of a 'fulfilled minister's wife'. Over the years she has carved out her role making good use of her strengths and giving her satisfaction and pleasure.

## Some points to consider

1. What have been major changes in your life? How have they affected you?

2. How do we define our 'destiny'? In what ways does it relate to that of our husband's calling? Is this a struggle sometimes?
3. What could be a useful help to ministers' wives in the way of life guidance and personal development?
4. How would you summarise your understanding of 'God's call' on your life at this point?
5. Are there new possibilities ahead? How can we find the support, advice and prayer-backing needed as we embark on this?

# 8. Peace Under Pressure

There was a certain place on my walk to church where I knew I had to pull myself together and dry my tears so as to arrive ready for the morning service with a suitably serene and jolly smile on my lips. I was so worried about my health problems and couldn't tell anyone how I really felt. But now looking back – with 20:20 hindsight! – God was at work in me in more ways than one and I'm actually even glad it all happened. (Anon)

## 'The pearl'

The pearl is first created when a grain of sand gets inside the shell of an oyster – or some other mollusc – which reacts to this discomfort by secreting a chemical that surrounds this irritating piece of grit. Layer by layer, more of this 'nacre' is laid down and the pearl grows in size, developing its own personality of irregular bumps and dents brought about by its unique environment. This silent miracle takes place secretly, hidden from view in the darkness, and the greater the irritant, the more beautiful the pearl becomes. Sometimes extra pressure inside the shell causes these layers to overlap, giving the pearl a special glow, making it even lovelier.

Pearls are soft and delicate living organisms, vulnerable to decay, acid and heat. They come in all shapes and sizes, in pink, black, white and even green. Every other jewel is cut and polished but a pearl just keeps growing, responding to its habitat until the day when it is lifted out of its environment to be displayed with others or placed alone in a gold or silver setting – for someone special perhaps. Unlike diamonds, which are almost indestructible, pearls needs loving care; they should be carefully washed and stored in protective box to keep them from harm.

John's vision of heaven comes right at the end of the Bible. It is an astonishingly lovely place that he tries to describe using earthly images. He writes

The twelve gates [of the city] were twelve pearls, each gate made of a single pearl.' (Rev. 21:21, NIV)

Imagine the moment when we will feast our eyes on those pearly gates! In the meantime we can marvel at the way God so often ordains great beauty to be created as a result of sustained pain under pressurised circumstances.

## Life under pressure

Dianne and Rob Parsons have been involved in the ministry of Care for the Family for many years. They are part of Glenwood Church in Cardiff, which formerly Rob led, simultaneously running a busy legal practice and giving seminars to other lawyers all over the country. It wasn't always easy, as Dianne shares here

Some years ago in Care for the Family we received an anonymous poem from a church leader's wife. I have read it many times but it always moves me.

I want my husband to smile again.
I want to be able to talk to him after dinner.
I want our family to go out on Saturdays for a walk or a shopping trip.
I want to be me – not 'the minister's wife'.
I want to sit in church, listen to the notices, and decide what *I would like to go to.*
I want my husband to come home at night and relax instead of just recharging the batteries and disappearing out again.
I want to celebrate birthdays and anniversaries always, not just when there are no church meetings.
I want to be able to tell the self-centred and self-righteous folk that they are.
I want him to come in at night and talk to us instead of slumping silently; reliving the awkward visit or difficult meeting he's been at.
I want people to stop telling me how wonderful it must be to be the minister's wife and then complain they've not had a visit for months.
I want people who regularly miss meetings because they've 'had a busy day' to let us miss occasional meetings because *we've* 'had a busy day'.
I want him to come with me sometimes to see our child swim or play football.
I want him to be my husband instead of their minister.
And I want not to be guilty about these things.

At the bottom of the poem is a PS: 'Tonight is one of those nights when it is all too much for me. I hope that you will read this, and maybe pray even though you don't know us.'

Perhaps it moves me so much because there was a period in our lives when I could have so easily identified with her feelings. We were in our early thirties (can it really be that long ago – it seems another lifetime!). We had two small children and after our second, Lloyd, was born I was ill for a number of years. My immune system crashed, my body ached so much I was unable to get up from bed and I had to get help to look after my children. That in itself made me feel very inadequate. But added to all of this was the fact that life was just so very busy. Rob would rush in from work, eat his meal on the run and then rush off to some meeting or other. To be honest I resented it a little that Rob seemed to have time for everybody except us. Rob is a brilliant husband, but he acknowledges now that those were difficult times; in fact he has written about those years in his books. I thank God that we learnt some deep lessons quickly so that by God's grace that time of turmoil was an *episode* in our marriage rather than a *lifestyle*.

I will never forget leading a discussion amongst church leaders' wives. In the question time a girl of about twelve put up her hand. She said, 'Why do I never see my father?' The really sad thing is that she wasn't being sarcastic; she seemed almost resigned to the fact that the man in her life just wasn't around very much.

I know that Christ calls us to love him more than our family but that cannot mean setting aside those for whom God has given us *primary* responsibility.

As I've said, we learnt some deep lessons during those times. Here are just a few:

1. *Learn to say no.* Although I bottled things up for a long time eventually I told Rob how our lifestyle was making me feel – and how I believed it had the capacity to destroy our family. To his great credit, Rob not only listened – he acted. I'm sure if you asked him now he would say that he gave up little that was truly necessary – he was still there for those who really needed him – but he learnt to say no a little more easily.

2. *Take practical steps to protect your home life.* Have periods during the evening when you are protected from the telephone. Whether it's putting the answer-

phone on, the mobile off, or pulling telephone plugs out – whatever it takes, *do it!*

3. *Don't feel guilty when you relax!* Encourage your husband to take his days off and protect them.
4. *Have some close friends* with whom you can let down the masks and have something to talk about other than the church.
5. *Don't spend your life wondering what other people are making of your parenting/prayer-life/hair.* There are tremendous pressures on the wives of church leaders to be the kind of women that others expect them to be. But although you are supportive of all that your husband is doing, God has given you gifts and a personality of your own. If you can't bake a cake to save your life, don't spend the rest of it trying to ice fairy cakes!
6. *Have topics of conversation with your husband other than the latest deacons' meeting or whether the PCC should alter the flower rota.* And even if you occasionally have a moan about some difficult person in your church, or the fact that the worship leader seems to have had a harmony bypass operation, try not to do that in front of your children; it will breed a cynical spirit in them.
7. *Laugh together.* I remembering saying to Rob many years ago, 'We don't laugh as much as we used to.' But we did recover those times of laughter and it's therapeutic!
8. *Forgive.* Let people off the hook as fast as you can. It is impossible to be involved in church

leadership without being hurt. I used to find that when people hurt Rob I would carry the pain longer than he did. But if possible, don't nurse it, don't gossip about it, just day by day and month by month ask God to help you let it go.

9. *Have a few friends with whom you pray regularly.* Life is hard and we need to draw on God. Give those weekly or monthly times priority.
10. *Encourage your husband.* I went through a period of my life where I thought that Rob got so much encouragement from others he didn't need it from me. But one day it dawned on me that he was more interested in what I thought more than anyone else in the world.

## Under pressure, over-pressurised?

There are times in our lives when it all feels too much. We are in good company. In 2 Corinthians 11:23-33 Paul lists a horrendous catalogue of troubles; from being flogged to getting shipwrecked. He describes nakedness, hunger, rejection – and on top of everything '... I face daily the pressure of my concern for all the churches. Who is weak and I do not feel weak? Who is led into sin, and I do not inwardly burn?' (NIV) He lived under pressure!

Christine Perkin owns a pressure cooker. She loves its versatility and the fact that in it you can prepare a casserole in less than half an hour and boil potatoes in under five minutes. In fact Christine became so impressed with this piece of kitchen equipment that she wrote a whole talk based on it! Here are some of her thoughts about pressure and stress

I realise it looks rather old-fashioned – like something from a World War Two exhibit! but basically a pressure cooker uses the build-up of pressure to cook things more effectively, and fast.

Coming into this life in the ministry can be a rapid learning curve – we've often to pick up skills and understand tricky situations in double-quick time. My experience was certainly this. I became a Christian at seventeen, was engaged at nineteen to a man who was about to be ordained, when I was barely twenty-one we married and went straight into our first parish. I felt so unprepared!

We inevitably see pressure as a negative thing; saying we are 'under a lot of pressure' as if things were pressing down on us, or 'over-pressurised' like a great wave was overwhelming us. But pressure cookers use the build up of pressure to their advantage; containing it, working with it and managing to produce good results out of it. Similarly, in our lives, pressure can focus us on a task, motivate us to keep going and challenge us to step out of our comfort zones. I wouldn't have attempted half of what I have if there hadn't been both external and internal pressure to do so. But there are some helpful truths I have learned from my aluminium culinary friend:

- *Secure the seal* – the rubber washer around the lid is one of the most important parts of the pressure cooker. If it isn't fitting properly – nothing works. In our lives we need the Holy Spirit's seal of his ownership and his approval.

- *Don't overfill* – otherwise the contents will overflow and make a dreadful mess. When we recognise our limitations and abide by them the pressure will not overcome us.

- *Set the timer* – otherwise the food will be either undercooked or completely mushy. In this job, timing is often everything. Time *off* in particular.

- *Adjust the temperature* – if the heat is full on throughout the cooking process it will not function properly. Take time to 'cool down' and relax.
- *Keep the lid on but let off 'controlled' steam* – opening the cooker mid-process would result in a bad scald but there is a little valve that safely releases the pressure. We need to be wise in the way we cope with our reactions to the stress we are under.
- *Enjoy the results* – although not every day in ministry is enjoyable, God wants us to take pleasure in what we do. We can be thankful for the blessings, his grace and for the privilege of serving him.

## Sharing burdens

Women married to church leaders are likely to be under pressure of many kinds. Pressure comes to us all in many guises; some of it is plain and obvious but at other times there's hidden pain that is difficult to share with others. Many cope with illness and disability, with problems relating to children and others in the family. Work pressures affect us and so do the problems within the church.

Diane Taylor writes

> Don't place unrealistic expectations on yourself. It is easy to feel somehow responsible for everyone in the church, and take on board their problems. I found, from hard experience, that the most useful phrase I could recite to myself was 'It's not my problem'. Once that fact was in place, I could be of far more use to people – able to help them but not 'go under' myself.
>
> In the early days of leadership, I hadn't learned one of life's key lessons: don't take on your husband's burdens – they are not yours to bear. Inevitably, church leadership leads to a considerable amount of criticism and unrealistic

> expectations from people. It is tempting, but fatal, to burden yourself with your husband's problems – you don't have the wherewithal to deal with those problems so, like a pressure cooker, your stress levels build up and there's nowhere for that stress to go.

The woman whose letter to Dianne Parsons appears above, was certainly loaded down with stress of many kinds. One area she alludes to is the pressure of church affairs on both her and her husband. Recently I received a letter from a minister's wife that raised the point Diane Taylor mentions above, writing: 'if as a married couple you want to be honest and share everything, isn't it right for a wife to know everything that has gone on in the elders' meetings or whatever? If this is not the case how can she properly support him?'

Alison Atkinson would say this

> Quite apart from time pressures, the work of the ministry can itself be stressful. Your husband may come home tired and weighed down by the demands of people and (even worse) church politics. Maybe you should resist the temptation to ask him to tell you all about it; there are things that are confidential which are better that you don't know about – and apart from anything else he's been dealing with it all day and would probably rather discuss something else with you. Some couples feel they have to share everything with each other but we have seen it put an undue strain on wives who may find their relationships with people in the church affected by things they don't need to know about.
>
> You will know in general terms when he's having a tough time, if the elders are getting him down again or if a complicated pastoral problem is threatening to overwhelm him. At those times, being especially loving, communicating your confidence and trust in him and

trying not to put extra demands on him will be a blessing – perhaps a romantic evening to take his mind off things would be a good idea.

There is a fine balance – and it will differ from couple to couple – between sharing everything and keeping important information and emotions back. Lyndon always reserves the right to tell me anything (with the assurance that it would go absolutely no further) but often chooses not to do so, to save me from unnecessary pain and pressure. I trust his judgement, and his right to decide this. Sometimes it is appropriate to tell me everything at a later date. On most occasions we do tell each other 'everything' but respect that this may not always be best and trust each other's judgement. This works both ways anyway – I certainly don't always tell Lyndon everything. We need wisdom about this, and discernment in choosing the right time to broach difficult issues personally or share the sad burdens and confidences of others.

Sometimes we fall into sin or undergo some experience that we feel is best kept a secret between husband and wife and not shared with friends – out of loyalty perhaps, or because we fear the consequences if the truth was discovered.

For many, money (or rather the lack of it) is a pressure. For others it is the sheer hard work of running church activities without adequate support and encouragement. The creating of pearl-like beauty in these situations is a hard process. I think it is very important to balance the reality of some of the problems in ministry with the pluses, the disappointing times with the joys. As they say in my church, 'God is good, *all* the time!' and he is waiting to hear our thanks, praise, requests and intercessions.

## Trusting God

The next chapter explores further what it is like when suffering comes. The apostle Paul went through so much in his ministry and he arrived at this conclusion

> Therefore I will boast all the more gladly about my weaknesses, so that Christ's power may rest on me. That is why, for Christ's sake, I delight in weaknesses, in insults, in hardships, in persecutions, in difficulties. For when I am weak, then I am strong.' (2 Cor. 12:9,10, NIV)

This is the crux of Christian ministry and it goes right against the wisdom of the world which says that success is what matters and that the most powerful, talented, beautiful and rich are the ones who matter most. God loves to bring about miracles through brokenness, peace through pain and victory through apparently ignominious defeat. Perhaps that can encourage us in the dark times, when we feel we have failed or that others have failed us. Ultimately it is in God we trust, in him alone.

Christine Freeland recalls a very painful period in the ministry she shared with David.

> I have not experienced the death of a partner, divorce or dismissal but 20 years ago we experienced the 'death' of our significant involvement in a vision so very dear to our hearts when we were left with a choice of two options which both seemed wrong. All I can say is that the Lord's mercy and grace have more than equalled the bewilderment and pain and we have come to trust him for what we still do not understand.
>
> Some problems are totally unexpected; others are almost predictable and I don't know which are harder to bear! Pastoral issues, theological issues, issues of relationships … and I have wanted to scream out, 'Not again, Lord!'

> Then every so often I see a situation beautifully develop into a nurturing discipling opportunity and I am at peace.
>
> I have learned to dread 'bitterness of spirit' taking root in my life at times of conflict and disappointment and I pray very specifically for deliverance from this natural but destructive reaction. I have come to understand the true meaning of 'sweetness' when in circumstances of hurt the Lord gives a deep assurance of love and tenderness. Just as the bitter water at Marah became sweet when Moses introduced the piece of wood (Exodus 15) so I have found the power of God to remove bitterness.

It is how we handle pressure that is important. Difficulties may well cause us to react in our naturally human way – that's how we are built! Emotions of anger, disappointment, self-pity, denial, anxiety etc. will threaten to dominate us. But as we find ourselves able to recognise God's eternal loving purposes and trust in all that lies ahead, it may be easier.

If worry is a sin – and I have a feeling it probably is – I need help as I worry often. It can debilitate us and distract us from trusting God. Paul understood this and suggested

> Don't fret or worry. Instead of worrying, pray. Let petitions and praises shape your worries into prayers, letting God know your concerns. Before you know it, a sense of God's wholeness, everything coming together for good, will come and settle you down. It's wonderful what happens when Christ displaces worry at the center of your life. (Phil. 4:6,7, *The Message*)

Achieving a state of ongoing calm is probably a lifelong process but I am determined to hold onto that wonderful peace more often in times of difficulty. Worry manifests itself in many ways but much of it is made worse when we are under too much stress.

Jesus Christ, King of glory.
Help us to make the right use of all the myrrh that God sends and to offer up to him the true incense of our hearts.

(Luke Johann Tauber 1300–61)

## Some points to consider

1. Maybe these Ten Commandments will help to put the circumstances and people who cause us pressure into perspective:

   *Ten Commandments for Reducing Stress*

   Thou shalt *not* be perfect, nor even try to be.
   Thou shalt *not* try to be all things to all people.
   Thou shalt leave things undone that ought to be undone.
   Thou shalt *not* spread thyself too thin.
   Thou shalt learn to say 'no'.
   Thou shalt schedule time for thyself, and thy supportive network.
   Thou shalt switch off, and do nothing regularly.
   Thou shalt be boring, untidy, inelegant and unattractive sometimes.
   Thou shalt *not* feel guilty.
   Especially, thou shalt *not* be thine own worst enemy, but thine own best friend.

2. What guidelines do you think are helpful for you as a couple when it comes to telling each other things?

3. What is the best way for you to relax when you are under pressure?

# 9. When Suffering Comes

After terrible upheaval, you may burn with anger – and then yearn so much for things to go back to how they once were. Eventually though, you will also turn – away from the hurt, and hopefully towards the One who loves you most, the source of resurrection, the source of hope. Each stage takes different lengths of time in different people, but each stage has to be experienced in true recovery. (Anon)

## 'The silversmith'

There was a group of women in a Bible study on the Book of Malachi. In Chapter 3 verse 3 it says: 'He will sit as a refiner and purifier of silver'. This puzzled the women and one of them offered to find out all about the process of refining silver and report back to the group next time. She tracked down a silversmith and made an appointment to visit his workshop to watch him at his craft. She didn't mention the reason for her interest.

She watched as the silversmith held a piece of silver in a flame and let it heat up. He explained that to refine silver one needed to hold the metal right in the centre of the fire where it was hottest so as to burn away all impurities. The woman thought of God holding us in such a hotspot from time to time but wondered again at the words of the verse 'He will sit as a refiner and purifier of silver'. When she asked the silversmith if he really had to stay sitting there in front of the fire the whole time the silver was being refined, he answered that yes, he not only must sit there holding the silver steadily but he needed to keep his eyes on it every second it was in there. For if the silver was left a moment too long in the heat it would be destroyed.

The woman asked one final question. 'How do you know when the silver is fully pure?' He smiled at her. 'That's easy! It's refined when I can see my reflection in it like a mirror.' (Anon. See http://www.clarion-call.org/extras/malachi.htm)

## … to become like his Son

There are no easy answers to suffering. Proverbs 17:3 says: 'The crucible for silver and the furnace for gold, but the LORD tests the heart.' (NIV) God does allow things to happen and those of us in positions of leadership will sooner or later be called upon to face difficult questions and gradually learn, in the midst of some form of suffering, secrets of how to find solace and security in God. Being in ministry doesn't exempt us from tragedy – although people sometimes seem 'surprised that God would let such things happen to good people'. Job 5:7 says: 'Yet man is born unto trouble, as the sparks fly upward' (KJV) and nobody knows what the future holds. We may have to face the loss of health, home, status, job or having to bear the pain and death of a loved one.

Paul, James and Peter all spoke about how this process is worked out in our lives as Christians.

> We can rejoice, too, when we run into problems and trials, for we know that they help us develop endurance. And endurance develops strength of character, and character strengthens our confident hope of salvation. And this hope will not lead to disappointment. (Rom. 5:3-5, NLT)

> Dear brothers and sisters, whenever trouble comes your way, consider it an opportunity for great joy. For you know that when your faith is tested, your endurance has a chance to grow. So let it grow, for when your endurance is fully developed, you will be perfect and complete needing nothing. (Jas. 1:2-4, NLT)

> Dear friends, don't be surprised at the fiery trials you are going through, as if something strange were happening to you. Instead be very glad – for these trials will make you partners with Christ in his suffering, so that you will have the wonderful joy of seeing his glory when it is revealed to all the world' (1 Pet. 4:12,13, NLT)

These scriptures tell us that suffering

- Develops character
- Allows us to be partners with Christ in his sufferings
- Makes us prove God's faithfulness
- Heaps up a harvest
- Equips us as we share with others.

I am very grateful that, compared with many, Lyndon and I have not been called to pass through too much in the way of suffering. Looking back at some hard experiences we have had, we genuinely thank God that they happened – even though they were very painful and sometimes frightening at the time. One that stands out is when I was diagnosed with a serious illness

> In October 1997, I noticed my fingertips were constantly tingling and within a week I had lost considerable strength in my hands and arms. Then my knees weakened and by the time I met the neurologist my GP referred me to I could scarcely walk and had lost sensation in various parts of my body. From being a super-active and fit person I was now reduced to holding the walls to move a few yards and in a permanent state of complete exhaustion. It was Multiple Sclerosis. I was forty-five years old.
>
> Somehow or other, God had prepared me for this. Some months earlier a very wise spiritual woman, Molly Dow, had spoken to me at a retreat we were both on with a group of other Christian leaders' wives. We had been singing the song – one of my favourites – 'Faithful One' (Brian Doerksen). When we had reached the part that says he lifts us up when we fall down, Molly looked across at me. God told her that I was going to fall down but he would not lift me up for quite a while. She courageously shared this 'encouragement' and prayed for me, and the memory of this occasion came right back as I sat in a hospital bed and wondered what on earth was going on. I knew I had to submit myself to God and place my trust in him and began to realise that even though I was in an un-get-outable pit, he was there with me. Not lifting me up at the moment but down in its murky depths with his everlasting arms around me.
>
> If only I could tell you about the outstanding spiritual journey the next year was for me! – but most of the time it was as much as I could do to squeak out the name of 'Jesus'. Once I was in a CT scanning machine – not a pleasant experience – and decided to recite some comforting scriptures to help me through. But I couldn't think of a single one and only just managed to stumble through the Lord's Prayer. I felt a complete failure as a Christian. Surely the 'when I am weak, he is strong'

theory meant I would burst out of the fetters of illness, triumphant over this horrible disease and able to amaze people with my spiritual insights and godly wisdom. A favourite Graham Kendrick song, 'In your way and in your time', kept me in many a dark moment.

I had my better days and on one of these I wrote a prayer which was later included in Louise Kendall's uplifting anthology that she wrote with her husband R.T. – *Great Christian Prayers* (London: Hodder and Stoughton, 2000).

Today I bought a walking stick.
O Jesus, it wasn't the happiest of purchases; dancing shoes would have pleased me better, but people with MS don't wear dancing shoes. Weak and weary, I need the stick to steady the same feet that used to whirl about to music
– such an exhilarating way to praise you; laughing and gasping to catch up with my own breath.

Lord, I still want to worship you.

As I stumble from the house with this crutch, you are there beside me and perhaps I'll see and hear you more distinctly than in the glorious flurry of dance.
There is always grace in every circumstance.
Please help me not to miss it. Amen.

I probably missed a lot of the grace God had for me because so often I felt so negative and cross and sorry for myself, but looking back I can see ways the whole experience changed both me and Lyndon. We learned truths we hadn't known existed and found value and delight in things we had just taken for granted before. And in his mercy God remarkably raised me up; I have had no residual signs of the disease since about 2001. We live in hope but recognise that nothing is certain. MS is an unpredictable condition, sometimes lying dormant for years, but at the time of writing I'm actually going to a Ball tomorrow evening, and definitely won't be taking a walking stick! God is so faithful.

Not everybody's story ends so happily – I am acutely aware of that. God does not always choose to heal and we rarely understand why. I know a young vicar's wife who has a terminal illness. She has to undergo continuous exhausting and painful treatment that is having a diminishing effect on her and her condition is getting worse. The prayer she asks is for God to give her 'just ten years, for my husband and the children'. I am so inspired by her courage in the face of such sorrow.

Marilyn Glass also speaks bravely in the light of the debilitating illness she contracted at about the time John was beginning a new phase of ministry as General Superintendent of the Elim churches.

> There is usually a cost when we start to 'move out' or 'move up'. The enemy is not pleased and often comes against us in any way that he can. Within a matter of weeks of us taking up our new role I faced a serious operation, had a fall in which I was concussed and suffered a broken wrist, and contracted a condition called fibromyalgia.
>
> Remarkably, despite this, I have found that this has brought me into a closer relationship with God and given me a greater compassion for others who have had to embrace similar circumstances.
>
> It never ceases to amaze me that, even in such situations, God allows his purposes to be worked out. He always gives the strength at the time it is needed most. There are times when I feel great and can travel at full speed and others when I am tempted to indulge in a pity party. The greatest tonic is the company and laughter of friends, and those around me that I love. It also helps to resolve

to focus on others rather than myself. As we endeavour to encourage others, God so often rewards the investment with an increase of his blessing into our own lives.

## God is faithful

From beginning to end, the Bible offers comfort and hope to individuals, groups and whole nations going through persecution, loss and tragedy. It persistently presents God as unfailingly faithful and good to his people even in the worst of times. None of us yet know how the whole story ends and all we can do when life makes no sense is, by faith, to trust him. In the Old Testament, Job in his darkest moments holds on to his deep commitment that

> Though he slay me, yet will I trust in him: but I will maintain mine own ways before him. (Job 13:15, KJV)

Ellie Leighton (not her real name) wrote the following about the period when she was coming to terms with her husband's affair

> That lovely phrase in the Authorised Version – 'it came to pass' was one of the golden nuggets that were God's presents to me in the darkest times. Situations come, and they pass. Impossible though it was to believe at the time, God reminded me that my situation would pass. In the meantime, there were certain precious life-lasting changes he could bring about in me if I would let him – but this was only possible in the blackness of the pit. When my present trial passed, the opportunity would too. He was right! My life has moved on and the lessons I learned in the darkness will enrich me for ever. But I possibly missed out on others because of my stubbornness and disbelief.

Habakkuk, although he questions God about why the wicked and violent of this world so often prosper at the expense of the poor, even causing devastation for God's people – concludes that God is just and will give strength to us in the midst of our suffering.

> Even though the fig trees have no blossoms, and there are no grapes on the vine; even though the olive crop fails, and the fields lie empty and barren; even though the flocks die in the fields and the cattle barns are empty, yet I will rejoice in the LORD! I will be joyful in the God of my salvation. The Sovereign LORD is my strength! He makes me as surefooted as a deer, able to tread upon the heights.' (Hab. 3:17–19, NLT)

I am silent before that kind of faith – it is way beyond my experience – but this very day thousands of brothers and sisters around the world are enduring the most terrible circumstances and living Habakkuk's testimony. In heaven, they will receive their reward; part of which will be to see how God used their experience and faith to bring about unexpected blessing to future generations.

## Heaping up a harvest

Lyndon and I recently came across the following inspiring story of a man who suffered in his lifetime but left an extraordinary legacy in the kingdom of God. The second century Christian writer Tertullian believed 'the blood of the martyrs is the seed of the church' and here surely is an example of that

> Ordained at the age of 24, Robert Thomas was an expert linguist and had also studied medicine. He joined the China Inland Mission and in 1864 embarked on a

hazardous voyage to China with his young wife Caroline. Tragically, their first baby, born shortly after their arrival, died – then Robert also lost his wife. Broken-hearted but undaunted he set out to carry the gospel to the 'Hermit Kingdom' of Korea. Heavily disguising himself and able to speak Korean he started distributing much-needed Bibles. However in 1866 at Phuong Pheng disaster struck when the trading vessel he was aboard was fired at from the riverbank. The entire crew were killed. Robert Thomas leapt overboard and swam to shore with his few remaining Bibles and frantically handed them out. He was caught, and immediately condemned to death. He humbly knelt down, begging the soldier to accept his last Bible, who hesitated for a moment before beheading the 27-year-old Thomas. His executioner later became a Christian.

For family and friends back home in Wales, Thomas's death was a tragic, needless loss. What they could not know then was that his martyrdom marked the beginning of a move of God that touched the world.

Any Korean found in possession of a Bible would be threatened with death, so pages were torn out to be used as wallpaper. People began to read the words out of sheer curiosity and were drawn to Christ. Twenty years later, others came to this place and were amazed to find a thriving church amid this previously unevangelised land.

Apparently every Korean Christian knows about Robert Thomas; he is revered as a spiritual father. Today Korea has twelve of the world's largest churches and missionaries from there have travelled all over the world with the gospel.

We all know how it feels to be downhearted and discouraged because our best efforts appear to be fruitless and our prayers seem unanswered. However, the Bible urges us not to give up but keep trusting that God's promise is sure that 'we will reap a harvest of blessing if we don't give up.' (Gal. 6:9, NLT) Our labours might be unseen and unacknowledged. The harvest of blessing we seek in our ministry situation may not be actually experienced by us but is for a future generation, as happened in Korea. But God sees, hears and never forgets.

(Adapted from a letter by Lyndon Bowring to CARE supporters, May 2005)

## Sharing our comfort

Facile answers don't help anybody in times of trouble; and more comforting than understanding 'why?' is discovering 'who' – what God will do to bring us through and how his strength can be a reality to keep us sane and safe in the midst of hardship, loss and pain when it hits us. And how he can use it all.

> 'Praise be to the God and Father of our Lord Jesus Christ, the Father of compassion and the God of all comfort, who comforts us in all our troubles, so that we can comfort those in any trouble with the comfort we ourselves have received from God. For just as the sufferings of Christ flow over into our lives, so also through Christ our comfort overflows. If we are distressed, it is for your comfort and salvation; if we are comforted, it is for your comfort, which produces in you patient endurance of the same sufferings we suffer. And our hope for you is firm, because we know that just as you share in our sufferings, so also you share in our comfort. (2 Cor. 1:3-7, NIV)

Davina Irwin-Clark wrote the following account of how God gave comfort in a time of family tragedy

> A curate's wife's pregnant tummy is public property! Everyone in our Yorkshire parish was thrilled to bits that we were expecting (I mean REALLY thrilled: we were given 34 hand-knitted baby jackets!!). Then I had the brilliance

to give birth on Sunday morning just in time for the lay-reader, also handily an obstetric consultant, to rush back to church and breathlessly announce her successful work of delivering a fat son into our arms! Sebastian arrived into the family of God as much as the Irwin-Clarks.

So the shock of his cot-death six weeks later hit everyone hard. And almost my first response as I cradled the little body came out of my wanting to bless and not harm that family in my grief. I remember so clearly praying 'Father I'm totally new to pain; I don't know how to do bereavement. They'll see my reactions and draw conclusions about you. What a responsibility! Please help. What should I do?' I very seldom hear God in a clear way, but then, unmistakably, he said '*I'm* not going to use the word ought, and you don't have to either.' That word made the whole difference to my relationship with the members of the church family over the next weeks. They were utterly lovely. They didn't say anything glib or insensitive, instead they hugged me and cried and said 'We just don't know what to say, but we love you.' Perfect. And because of God's release, I didn't feel I had to react in any particular way, or keep my grief private, or indeed share it, or give teaching from it. I could simply let the reality of grief's waves wash up and down, and let God heal me without the extra pressures of getting it 'right' as a leader's wife.

Our rector preached on 'he comforts us in all our troubles so that we can comfort others' and that was one of the grace-filled results of Sebastian's death. But before the comfort came identification. Many people it seemed, though fond of us, (they said) had us on a pedestal, and could hardly imagine that we lived 'normal' lives. But when this hit us and everyone could see how appalling it was, the gap between us disappeared. They identified with our pain and confusion, and let us into theirs as never before.

I'll always remember Joan – I'd always been scared of her. In her seventies (I was twenty-six), she was the parish organiser, and was often cross, so I confess I'd scuttle down one aisle as she advanced up another! But then she came to coffee after Sebastian died. Of course she had that Yorkshirewoman's honesty and told me. 'To tell ye the truth, you've stuck in my gullet.' Our southern ways, our Volvo, our easy family life and permanent smiles had been dreadful for her. She told me her story of having lost a desperately-wanted baby 50 years before. Joan's husband had made one remark: 'We'll say nowt more about it.' And he never had. So of course I realised then that all the scary crossness had been buried pain; I saw the young mum inside her, and we cried bitterly together. And then she said 'Well now it's happened to you, and not all your education or your double-barrelled name could stop it. But what I want to know is, do you still believe God is loving?' And so, because of my own loss, she was able to hear me as I wept and told her of our Father God who had also lost a Son and therefore knew exactly what we were suffering. I can't say what a depth of comfort came to both of us from the reality of sharing God's own comfort that day.

Although she has experienced many instances of God's grace and comfort in the midst of their ordeal, one mother writes with heartfelt raw honesty about her less positive experience of the people in their church – and the struggle she had to get through her deep pain

It was different before Edward was born. Although I had times when I wanted to throw the chip-eating teenagers off my sofa arms and would think longingly of dropping my one- and two-year-olds off with moaning single friends for 24 hours, I was able to laugh at the frustrations.

Then, following a difficult pregnancy our third son came and I was shoved, still wearing my dressing-gown, into the barbaric world of heart surgery, intensive care and dying children. Instead of being wrapped in fine cotton and held close, he lay paralysed and naked, his eyes taped down and his face distorted with wires and tubes. Only his fingers remained as before, and he clasped my finger as I sat on the stool staring at his heart straining under the cellophane. Some members of our church came; there were cards but no flowers. The people whose lives we had poured ourselves into didn't really show and apart from family, just three or four people cared for us. For the first couple of weeks it didn't matter. We were oblivious. I was told they prayed for us. Finally, we rang the leadership team and suggested that they got themselves in to Great Ormond Street Hospital and pray with us. It seems crazy but I will never forget those who cared – and those who didn't.

Finally released several months later we tried to get our life back. The problem was, our lives were ministry, and I was unpleasantly shocked at the impatience and anger I felt towards our congregation. My son was still critically ill. He required round-the-clock care and terrifyingly stopped breathing several times a day. I was also unwell and supposed to have had surgery immediately following Ed's birth but couldn't as it required six to eight weeks bed rest – impossible. But the people in our church were still ready to off-load their cares of the past six months so the door-bell and phone started ringing, the coffee was made and counsel was given. What happened to me? I was lost in a world of ragged scars and searing pain. I didn't really pray, just pleaded for the life of my baby. Six years and seven operations later I still hurt like crazy and much of my praying is pleas for mercy. There is no cure for my son's illness. We have been told that he may not make it past primary school. We can't say goodbye to the hospital waiting room and unless God miraculously heals Ed, he has a painful future.

Being the mother of a sick child and a pastor's wife is not an easy co-existence. Both Christians and non-Christians have incredibly high standards for me that include being available and having a smile, not to mention perfect kids, a great marriage, a constant supply of wholesome meals – all this with no money and little sleep. Perhaps I'm bitter but I don't think so.

Looking at death produces a grim reality. I think our churches generally lack love. Too many people are out for what they can get and this does affect us pastors' wives. What is truly wonderful and makes my day every time is when I *am* loved, through a smile, an appreciation, a hug, a gift, a break. My 'faith' has not weakened, quite simply because God has loved me so significantly. He doesn't seem to mind my pleas, my anger. Perhaps because he knows the pain of watching a beloved son die.

## Taking our pain

Living in a fallen world means that suffering is unavoidable, and although we cry out for ourselves and for others that God would mercifully deliver us out of bad painful situations, sometimes he does not do this. If like Susanna, in amongst the questions, disappointments and near-despair, we can reach a place of knowing God's love in the depth of our being, we have something that *will* bring us through the night.

Jesus knew hunger, tiredness and thirst. He was bereaved, let down and made to face cruel and corrupt opposition from the very religious leaders who might have been expected to embrace him. Jesus ended up on the cross, utterly defeated – and yet Calvary's apparent catastrophe was completely reversed at the resurrection.

> For God caused Christ, who himself knew nothing of sin, actually to *be* sin for our sakes, so that in Christ we might be made good with the goodness of God. (2 Cor. 5:21, J.B. Phillips)

I did some more research into the process of silver refining. I found out that when the raw silver ore – still mixed up with particles of rock and other bits of dirt – is placed in the crucible, lead is also added. Lead has the unusual property of absorbing impurities into itself. As the heat intensifies in the furnace and everything melts together, the contaminated lead begins to rise to the top. This worthless dross is then blown over the edge into the flames below, leaving the silver that much more pure.

In a similar way, Jesus took our sin into his own body on the cross, 'becoming sin', that we might be released from the curse of death, and set free from the power of sin to live forever.

## Some points to consider

1. While we are going through it, how can we try to receive God's promises – of his presence, his comfort, and that good *can* come out of what is happening?
2. Can we think of people whom we could comfort as a result of going through a similar trial ourselves?
3. Looking back on the painful times, are there areas of unresolved hurt that we believe God might heal? How, when and with whose help could we explore this?

# 10. When the Unthinkable Happens

Put your energy, time and effort in the meantime, into building up your marriage. Why would the devil want to invest his time and resources into spoiling diverse bits and pieces of ministry, when he could bring the whole church crashing down in one go by destroying the pastor's marriage? (Anon)

## 'Footprints'

One night I had a dream. I dreamed I was walking along the beach with the Lord and across the sky flashed scenes from my life. For each scene, I noticed two sets of footprints in the sand, one belonging to me, and one belonging to the Lord. When the last scene of my life flashed before us, I looked back at the footprints in the sand. I noticed that at times along the path of my life, there was only one set of footprints. I also noticed that it happened at the very lowest and saddest times of my life. This really bothered me and I questioned the Lord about it. 'Lord, you said that once I decided to follow You, You would walk with me all the way but I noticed that during the most troublesome times in my life there is only one set of footprints. I don't understand why, in

> times when I needed You most, You would leave me.' The Lord replied, 'My precious, precious child, I love you and I would never, never leave you during your times of trials and suffering. When you saw only one set of footprints, it was then that I carried you.'
> (Margaret Fishback Powers)

I have endeavoured to make this book real. By including others' stories, their candid observations and heartfelt yearnings I sincerely hope you the reader can identify with other women's experiences and be encouraged in your own journey. Over years of involvement with Christian leaders' wives through the ministry of Living with Leadership and in researching and writing this book, I have come across many instances of pain, often alongside great enthusiasm, encouragement and enjoyment. There is so much all woven in together. And the golden thread through it all is the faithfulness of God. Our lives are entwined with him and when trouble comes we face a stark choice – do we choose to trust him, or not?

## Adversary

In every challenge facing us we are reminded of the reality of what Ephesians 6 describes as a spiritual battle against a vicious, deceitful foe – described by Jesus like this

> He always was a murderer, and has never dealt with the truth; since the truth will have nothing to do with him … he is a liar and the father of lies.
> (Jn. 8:44, J.B. Phillips)

As volunteer foot soldiers in the King's army, from time to time we are inevitably susceptible to fear, opposition, injury and even death. Peter, who had been targeted often enough by Satan warned believers about him

> Be sober, be vigilant; because your adversary the devil walks around like a roaring lion, seeking whom he may devour. Resist him, steadfast in the faith … (1 Pet. 5:8,9, NKJV)

It is important for anyone in leadership to have a right and balanced view of the devil; aware and wary of his evil intentions and capabilities yet confidently relying on Christ's complete victory over him; that as Paul put it: 'the God of peace will crush Satan under your feet shortly.' Romans 16:20 (NKJV)

It would be wrong to blame the devil for the consequences of our sins, but wherever he can get a foothold, he will. It is a sad fact that increasingly, married couples in ministry roles are experiencing difficulties – sometimes as a consequence of adultery. For some there is a path back through forgiveness and repentance but a significant number of marriages are ending in divorce while other couples struggle to keep up appearances and hide their pain from others. I recently met two women whose husbands had left them. They have allowed me to include their stories (not under their own names – details are changed to protect their identities). I think it is important to face such a subject in this book for two reasons. One, because the unthinkable *does* happen and *may* happen to someone we know, or even ourselves. Knowing others have gone through it may offer comfort to someone. Secondly, reading about Ellie and Lou will provide insight in the event of our needing to help another woman going through a similar experience – and this is what they both strongly desire. In fact both have said they would willingly make themselves available to listen and talk if ever this was needed. (Please contact publisher for further information.)

## Ellie's story

It could never happen to me. But it did.

It happened to me on a Monday morning when my husband calmly announced at the breakfast table: 'There's something we need to talk about.' Yesterday, the earth remained horizontal – I joined in the worship songs, prayed and listened, I talked to people after the service, invited someone for lunch. My husband's sermons proved unusually brief, and uninspired, but then his preaching had lost its vital spark some time ago, so nothing dramatic warned me that normality was about to explode. No inkling that next Sunday I would have no church to go to, or that like an unsuspecting foetus at the moment of abortion, I was about to be ripped from the warmth of the womb, and thrown out into a cold wet field to fend alone.

My husband had had an affair, and been found out. He would have to resign from ministry, so have no job, no career, no money, no home at a time when the children were in the throes of GCSEs and A-levels. Worst of all, he didn't know whether he loved me or not and couldn't decide whether he was leaving me or staying.

Ten minutes on a Monday morning blasted me out of my orbit to change my life for ever. It couldn't happen to us. My husband was a gifted preacher who had been in ministry for twenty years, led many people to the Lord, preached countless sermons on Christian living and spiritual growth. He was a down-to-earth man who knew the pitfalls inside out. It couldn't have happened to us. But it had. And it will happen to others.

We all think we are beyond temptation in that particular area, yet the truth is the devil seldom attacks well-defended ground, but seeks out our weakness, insidiously probing and endeavouring to gain a toehold at our vulnerable spot. Pray for vision and wisdom and self-awareness, keep on praying for protection and don't let your guard down for an instant. Equip yourself with an army of friends who will surround your marriage with prayer.

There had never been a time throughout my twenty-year marriage, when I had so desperately craved my husband's tender love and care, so urgently needed to pour out my anguish to him, and know that we were standing solidly together. But at this horrific moment of pain, the loving support of my husband was abruptly whipped away, along with almost every other support and security I had ever known. In every other crisis your church would gather round you and encircle you with love but for the first time in 50 years, I found myself in the unimaginable place of no church to go to on Sunday and without the comfort and assurance of being physically surrounded by a loving church family.

In fact, I do want you to know that the leadership and church members proved themselves to be 'friends closer than a brother', and cared for me. It is a tribute to their Christ-likeness that I am once again in the fellowship of that church, part of the family. But for a time I had to face the stark reality and loneliness of being outside the church family, with no place in its gatherings, discussion or activities. This brought pain beyond expression and I dreamed of the ancient barbaric custom of being burned alive on my husband's funeral pyre.

My own story has many complex threads and twists, culminating in my husband leaving the family home, and subsequent divorce. My journey continues and I would best describe it in the words of a lovely song, that God will lead me by a roadway in the wilderness and that in the desert I will see rivers.

A desert path it certainly has been; barren, lonely and hard going. The scenery is often bleak and monotonous with few signposts along the way indicating how far you still have to travel. I hadn't a clue what form the Promised Land might take, but I knew that was where the track led. Many times he's had to remind me that it is a pathway I'm on, not a motorway, on foot, not eating up the miles in a Ferrari. You can't rush the business of healing, there are no shortcuts. I am learning to let the Lord take his time with me.

What I searched for, unsuccessfully, was a book written to address the host of problems and extra pain specific to the wife of a minister. Perhaps my failure reflects the fact that the situation poses so many intricate problems with so few answers. However, *Missing Being Mrs* by Jennifer Croly [*Missing Being Mrs: Surviving Divorce Without Losing Your Friends, Your Faith, Your Mind,* Kregel Publications] reflected much of my own emotions and experiences, and enabled me to climb further up the learning curve of coming to terms with the loss of my husband.

God never said life would be easy. He never said life would be fair. He never said other people would not destroy what you had built, or that robbers would not break in to steal and destroy. He never promised that after the thieves had robbed you, you would get your belongings back. He did not promise lives free of the consequences of other people's sin, or that you would not end the day so tired that you could barely stand. There are no assurances in Scripture that this will not continue day after day. I wish there were, but there aren't.

But he has promised me strength for today, hope for tomorrow and when tomorrow dawns, strength for that day too. He has promised wisdom if I ask. He has said he will work for my best in all things, to nurture and sustain me, to provide for my needs and fulfil his purpose for my life. I believe he will stay with me, guide and lead me, and turn me away from wrong paths. He will place a light burden on me in place of sin's heavy one, will stay yoked to me and prevent me being burned up in the fire or drowned in the flood. If I stay faithful, he has promised great reward in heaven and abundant life now. He will use me to love others. He will remain unchanging, be my rock and fortress, shelter me under his wings, hold me close, and never fail or forsake me!!

I still have problems, questions remain without answers and sometimes I still slither into the 'slough of despond'. But God always picks me up again and sets me back on solid ground. His joy and his peace rob the shadows of their power to destroy.

My testimony is, that not only is it possible to survive this experience, but under God's hand, to flourish. Three years back, on that darkest of Monday mornings, my troubled soul would have said 'that could never happen to me.' But it has.

One of the blessings that has come to Ellie is unexpected friendship. The denomination to which she belongs has sought to support women in her predicament and as a result she was introduced to Lou (not her real name) who tells her story here. These two women are part of a support group and are asking God to show them ways to reach out to other women in similar situations.

## Lou's story

It's been years now, since my husband called time on our marriage, our family and his ministry for the sake of an affair with a woman I thought was a friend. It took at least ten of those years before I could wake up in the morning without a feeling of total incredulity that this should have happened to me. Me! The golden girl in the church youth group who followed the Lord all the way to Bible school, found love there, and fell for a good bloke as deeply as it's possible to do. Mission then called and though it wasn't easy to leave homeland and family, I followed my husband as he followed the Lord and as the kids came along, we made a tight little unit.

We came home after seven years so Neil could pursue a university degree. I was intensely proud of him and worked part time to support his studies while we cared for our growing children together. After graduation, a city church approached us and though steeped in tradition, people were anxious to follow God and grow in worship and learning. Little did I know that at our induction service a woman sat in the congregation who would help cripple my marriage, devastate my children's lives, and end a fruitful ministry.

When 'Alicia' approached us for counselling my husband sensed something awry and said 'we must counsel her together – I feel alarm bells ringing.' He was right. After some months, she told us she felt better, but without my knowing, asked Neil to continue seeing her alone. He did so, keeping it secret from me and this was the beginning of something crumbling from the inside.

I can honestly say that although I noticed Neil's attitude 'toughening up' in the way he dealt with people in general and us too it never once occurred to me that he might be turning into a fallen angel. I knew there was something different, but dismissed it as being due to mid-life crisis or problems with the church. He decided to resign and told me later that he had tried to end his affair then, as he had on a number of other occasions. Yet, at our farewell – being in total ignorance of this at the time – I hugged Alicia without a second thought and cried buckets! After all, she'd been part of our house group and worship group and we had often socialised as families. I knew she and Neil got on well, I just didn't know how well!

As we breathed in the good air of a country posting, I prayed it would signal a new beginning. Neil's ministry took off, the church began to grow, and for a while, I felt we were back on track. Soon however, life began to unravel at home, and though I could never share it with anyone in the church, I told my best friend (who was also in ministry) that I was deeply worried. I noticed that away from the church and other commitments, Neil was increasingly snappy with the kids and often also with me.

'What is the matter with you these days?' I asked. 'You're always angry, you won't talk to us – if I didn't know you better, I would think you were having an affair!' 'That's not the problem!' he snapped back, and clammed up. I didn't for one moment actually think he *was* having an affair – I just wanted him to talk to me.

We carried on throughout the spring and summer but life was not good and I began to think he might be ill – he'd changed so much. He preached a startlingly effective sermon on marriage, and it was the only time in our own relationship I ever remember telling him that I desperately wished he would practise what he preached.

Then the first bomb dropped. Our youngest daughter had been staying with a friend near our old church, when she saw her dad's car parked in a road adjacent to Alicia's. She called to tell me, obviously not realising the significance of the location but wanting to know why her dad hadn't contacted her. I told her that he was elsewhere, but she was adamant that it was his car, also adding that there was a copy of a certain magazine in the back. I managed to diffuse her concern, but suddenly, in some strange way, everything fell into place. Unaccountably, Alicia's name had been going round in my head for months. Instinct? Warning? Who knows? (All I do know is that I've learned to trust my instincts far more, and it's been a good choice!)

When Neil came home well after midnight, I challenged him with our daughter's sighting, which he denied, getting angry when I pressed the case. I got up early next day, found the magazine in his car and with a sinking heart, presented him with it. The blood drained from his face. I told him he had to talk to me, that at the very least he owed me that, but he drove off angrily, straight to Alicia.

That evening, he spun what was later to prove a web of lies, saying that the affair had grown from counselling but had never become intimate. Though I was desperately hurt, I knew there was no way I wanted to end my marriage – I still loved him too much. In actual fact, as I later discovered, the story he had told so convincingly was a cover that he and Alicia had planned to tell their spouses if they ever became suspicious. Then came the second bomb. Alicia's husband (far more worldly wise than me) became suspicious that she was having an affair, so tapped their phone – and heard a conversation between her and Neil which spelt things out as they really were. Alicia's husband was astonished. He had a long list of suspects, but Neil's name was never on it!

As soon as I knew the truth, I threw him out. Later when I went to put a bag in the dustbin, I discovered he'd thrown something out too – all his clerical collars, and the wedding ring I had given back to him. With it went our marriage, his good relationships with his children, family and closest friends – with almost everyone in fact, he had once held to be the dearest in his life. I believe it's called 'The expulsive power of a new affection'.

Some time previously, at Neil's insistence, I'd blithely signed our pensions into his sole name. It took a while for the truth to dawn, but many similar issues came to light which made me realise how very naive I had been – not to mention how well stitched up!

We didn't own a home, so the only financial issue to settle was that month's salary, which the church divided between us. I made plans to vacate the manse, and despite one terrible moment when the Citizens Advice Bureau confirmed I was a hopeless case, the good Lord intervened in a miraculous way to put a roof over our heads and food on the table – something he's been doing ever since.

I faced lots of local fall-out. Our children were utterly heartbroken and just couldn't believe what had happened. They had to go back to school where everyone knew

Neil – he had spoken in assembly just a few short weeks before. Some in our fellowship who had loved and respected him deeply, asked me whether they needed to have their children re-dedicated, or go through their marriage counselling again, and everywhere I turned, there were reminders of his failure which by default, had become mine also. It was bereavement without honour.

I found it impossible to worship and went into intense depression. At one point, I phoned my sister, a bottle of anti-depressants in my hand and asked her to give me one good reason why I shouldn't take them all. She gave me three good reasons – the names of my children. The pills got flushed. I owe my friends and family so much.

Time and time again, God stepped in through so many wonderfully vibrant and different people. They were his arms and legs, his wallet and heart, his talents and joy in our lives. They hugged us, supported us with their time, encouraged us with their jokes and laughter and loved us unconditionally. They helped us put one foot in front of the other.

The kids and I went through desperate times. Every electrical appliance in our adopted house broke down; we endured floods in the kitchen, boiler breakdown (no heat for 18 months), several redundancies, car crashes, and problems with drugs, boyfriends and bullying. Yet through it all, the good Lord preserved us. Times were dire, but they were also precious. 'Treasures of darkness' the Scripture calls them – treasures which forge our relationships into something strong and bright and brilliant.

Looking back, my own sins were those of omission. I saw the signs and misinterpreted them, thinking he was ill, or stressed, or going through some mid-life crisis. Maybe I didn't snoop enough, or blindly trusted too much. Maybe I didn't let him know how deeply he was loved and appreciated. The truth is, I never had a chance to address any issues that may have been wrong between us. In his resignation letter to the church, he said it wasn't my fault. In the end, I've always been content to let God be the judge.

Many 'bless and burn' memories wing their way to me still: songs we sang, Scripture we loved, sermons he preached, great times we had together, with our children and our friends – deep moments of the soul, late night discussions and lots of fun. I don't believe for one second that the sweetness of such a walk with God can so easily be dismissed.

As for me, I'm no plaster saint and haven't made a particularly good job of discipleship but I know that the resurrection of Jesus and the life he offers brings hope beyond compare. Though I stumble and fall all the time, I keep getting up and do my best to hang in there, behind the Shepherd.

Bad things happen, and the best of people can let you down, but whatever your circumstances, *never* underestimate how important you are to your family – even if they don't tell you often enough and you sometimes feel taken for granted. In the real world, some marriages will end in troubled circumstances but *how* they end is important – how you do what you do, especially to those who love you most, is desperately important.

# 11. Taken Away

'And we know that in all things God works for the good of those who love him, who have been called according to his purpose.' This is a truth I see played out every day and never more so than since my husband Ron died in 2002. They are words that can seem almost hurtful in the deep mourning time and yet I know now that from the beginning God was preparing me for this loss and sowing into me a capacity to cope. Step by step he guided and step by step he provided. (Anon)

## 'The bamboo tree'

Far away and in the midst of a barren patch of countryside there was a beautiful garden. Among the plants was a tall and handsome bamboo tree, lovingly tended by the master of the house. The tree knew it was strong and tall, and loved its master greatly for tending it. He longed to show his love and commitment, and one day asked 'Master, how can I serve you more?'

The master gently placed his hands of the bamboo and replied tenderly: 'by allowing me to cut down your branches.'

Horrified the tree protested – 'Surely you don't mean that! Everybody knows I want to serve you more – but however can I serve you as a tall tree if my branches are cut down?'

'Not only must I cut down your branches, but strip them naked. Your tallest shoot I must cut in half so as to scoop out your heart,' said the master.

The tree was truly shocked now, but because it loved and trusted the master so much, humbly submitted. It was stripped down of branch and leaf, the strongest shoot was cut right through the middle and the fleshy insides were scooped out.

Then an extraordinary thing happened. The master laid end-to-end these two halves, hollowed out and cleaned to create a very long open pipe. He laid one end where the crystal clear spring water gushed out and because the pipe was so long it stretched outside the garden right into the barren area beyond. Some of the precious water now started to flow into the new pipe – slowly at first then more strongly – and it was clear that for many years the strongest, tallest, proudest shoots of the bamboo would go on serving as a life-giving conduit bringing water to places that had never been irrigated before. (A traditional story from China)

Every branch that does bear fruit he prunes so that it will be even more fruitful. (Jn. 15:2b, NIV)

## Hazel's story

This chapter describes one woman's experience of becoming a widow. Her story is poignant and also overflowing with hope. It is filled with examples of how God has provided and brought good out of this human disaster.

One of the best ministry 'double-acts' around, Dave and Hazel Marchment worked for many years with the people of Basingstoke Community Church, part of

Salt and Light ministries. They both exercised pastoral, teaching and leadership gifts and served the Lord in a variety of ways, enjoying a close, loving marriage and family life and as the children got older, finding increasing opportunities to extend their borders to far-flung parts of the world. I was acquainted with Hazel then but, as I have come to know her, my admiration and respect for her has deepened more and more. Her faith in God is remarkable; he is constantly at work in and through Hazel as she reaches out to others – including ministers' wives. I am grateful for her writing this; the story of what happened.

> I knew something was terribly wrong when I found Dave curled up in a foetal position on top of our bed. Generally so energetic and full of life, he'd not made the journey to get right under the duvet. Subconsciously I realised I'd been deeply concerned for some months without being able to articulate it. Life appeared normal; we were speaking together in churches and retreats and Dave was as active as usual with his responsibility as a senior pastor.
>
> Now we discovered that Dave's heart valve was so infected that it could detach at any moment, so we needed to be instantly ready to journey to London's Royal Brompton Hospital for heart surgery. Afterwards high doses of antibiotics were injected to reduce the infection, and Dave was taken straight into coronary care.
>
> I remember saying to a doctor, 'You need to do everything possible for him – he's known and loved by thousands of people!' She graciously agreed and of course I realised that each patient is treated with equal care as far as possible. That care transpired to be exemplary and I have only the utmost gratefulness and respect for the NHS. Truly devoted doctors and nurses surrounded us and they were so aware and considerate towards ... us as we tried to come to terms with the diagnosis.

The three of us (me, our daughter Cara and son Carl) felt we needed support that night. We were in shock, but somehow peaceful as prayer-chain messages resulted in immediate support and we began to receive from God what I've only really heard about in books! A peace impossible to describe began to be our companion. It didn't by-pass all the emotional trauma but it superseded it as we tried to come to terms with how seriously ill Dave was.

The prayer, financial, emotional and practical support at this time of crisis was unbelievable. In the past we had helped many others through difficult times in their lives but we were now the recipients; deeply in need of people who cared and understood the huge impact of isolation and the neuropathic effects of chemotherapy. Dave had to be kept away from every single form of infection or any opportunity for harmful bacteria to even touch his body.

I'd said to God on various occasions 'You've chosen the wrong person for this, Lord!' I had always felt very inadequate and far too sensitive to face difficult times, especially if that meant having to watch people's suffering. Each day, walking into the hospital, I would find myself saying 'I haven't got it, Lord. Please give me your strength and grace' and in the most tangible and extraordinary way he did! At that place of total vulnerability he was there for me, pouring in the strength and grace I needed. Dave and I prayed continually, 'Please fill us today with your life, Lord.' Even in the middle of heart monitors, blood transfusions, injections, plastic aprons and separation that's what God did; to such a degree that we lived in a huge amount of normality during those three years. It was a time of experiencing the depth of God in a way which isn't known except in very challenging times.

Many people prayed for Dave during the time of his illness. We all interceded that God would heal him and many miraculous answers encouraged us along the way, with infections rapidly subsiding and medical procedures allowed to became more straightforward. But we weren't given the ultimate miracle. I am so grateful that underneath our prayers, all miraculous intervention and our great desire, we have the bedrock of God's sovereignty.

From being a very busy leader's wife doing the many things that this involves and loving it, overnight I'd become a carer. In retrospect I wouldn't have chosen any other path. Everything is filtered for us by God's hand and I needed his continual strength to become a person that wasn't naturally me!

Through all this my passion for honouring each individual person that God gives us grew and grew. I found God capable of bringing light even into the most profound darkness. So much light in fact, that in remembering those days, it is not with deep regret or even overwhelming sorrow, but with complete gratefulness to a God who has proved that his promises of faithfulness and provision are there for all of us.

How God can strategise so wonderfully is a constant mystery, but he has poured that kind of detailed care into our lives. Despite their different ages, Cara and Carl both went to University in Bath at the same time, so travelling to have family time has been easy and successful. He hasn't missed a detail; proving to me how his heart is truly full of care for widows, and all who experience loss.

I've drawn many encouragements from the book of Job. Previously I'd wondered if this book was in the Bible by mistake as it seemed so thoroughly miserable! However I have recently called Job 'my friend' and learnt so much from different aspects of his life. Probably the first Bible book ever written, it has been a source of valuable depths of insight to help us in our journey through suffering. I'm sure Job would be amazed to know that this desperate season of his life, his response to it and God's faithfulness in it would ricochet down through the centuries spurring many on to face tragedy with a heart lifted to heaven in spite of unspeakable sorrow.

Job's winter season seemed particularly harsh but it is a delight when we read that the summer returned into his life again. He'd come face to face with God and his power. He'd done what so many of God's people have, following in his footsteps, allowing God to transform and reshape them. There's a certain depth, richness, beauty and holiness about a life that's walked along the unchosen path.

It's so important to stand with each other through 'Job experiences'. After all, we don't really know what may be going on in heaven that will initiate the events in our lives!

## Some points to consider

1. Are there any practical considerations to think about now, in case of the premature death of my husband?
2. Do I know anyone who has been bereaved who needs encouragement? Are there ways I can be a comforting friend?
3. How would I react to God if something like this happened to me?

# 12. Walking with Jesus

Where do I draw my spiritual strength from? When I'm walking in the countryside most of all; I can pray then and enjoy the utter peace and quiet. But from day to day – I listen to worship tapes, read a fair number of Christian books and get a lot out of church services. (Fortunately I really like my husband's preaching!) (Anon)

## Following the Shepherd

The Lord is my Shepherd – *that's Relationship!*
I shall not want – *that's Supply!*
He makes me to lie down in green pastures – *that's Rest!*
He leads me beside the still waters – *that's Refreshment!*
He restores my soul – *that's Healing!*
He leads me in he paths of righteousness – *that's Guidance!*
For his name's sake – *that's Purpose!*
Even though I walk through the valley of the shadow of death – *that's Testing!*
I will fear no evil – *that's Protection!*
For you art with me – *that's Faithfulness!*
Your rod and staff, they comfort me – *that's Discipline!*
You prepare a table before me in the presence of mine enemies – *that's Hope!*

You anoint my head with oil – *that's Consecration!*
My cup runs over – *that's Abundance!*
Surely goodness and mercy will follow me all the days of my life – *that's Blessing!*
And I will dwell in the house of the Lord – *that's Security!*
Forever – *that's Eternity!*
(Source unknown)

The twenty-third psalm has inspired God's people throughout the ages. It is so applicable to every situation. I love to reflect on the imagery of still waters, green meadows and paths of righteousness that speaks to our deepest spiritual longings. When I feel stressed and anxious, the reminder of his rod and staff to protect and guide, and his table and cup of plenty to provide our needs even in the direst times of attack, revives my hope. And his anointing oil symbolically consecrating and commissioning us to serve Jesus shows just how much he treasures each one of us.

## Time to pray

I remember listening to Davina Irwin-Clark speak on Psalm 23 and here she writes about how it helped her in her efforts to 'maintain a spiritual life' as a busy mum.

Two different godly women made an impact on me in my early years as a mother and clergy wife. The first, a clergy widow, wrote me a note containing verses about his 'leading gently those who are with young' and went on, brimming over about God's delight in me as his child, his support of me in my struggles to be the best mother ever(!) and his understanding of why I seldom managed a classic Quiet Time. That 'shepherd' concept was so comforting as I often felt I didn't make much sense or pray 'properly'. I just curled up in his arms and as often as not fell straight asleep instead of concentrating! But there was no condemnation, and somehow I knew he would hold my hand even when the grip the other way round wasn't all that tight.

Then I went on a clergy retreat. The speaker, a lovely woman, described how every morning she would go up to a special room set aside in the house for her times with God. There she would lie on the floor and simply soak in his presence, and this provided the strength and direction for the day. It was intended as encouragement and there was no question of the lovely effect of the Spirit's work in her – she shone as if the transfiguration happened every morning in her eyrie. But comparing this with my own bleary starts to the day I felt condemned. The only times I lay on the floor was to look for Lego under the sofa! And the thought of getting up even ten minutes earlier at that stage was agony. Anyway just how early would that be, to be ahead of a startlingly active three-year-old?!

Sadly, that cloud of self-reproach lasted quite a while. In fact I got stuck in a cycle of not praying for too long, and then feeling I simply couldn't pray in the ten minutes available because there wouldn't be time to repent of all my laziness, ill-discipline etc.! Guilt isn't a good motivator and as if I had spent weeks trailing off into the desert, I felt a similar amount of time would be needed to trudge back. There was neither energy nor time for that to be possible. But then I remembered the Shepherd, and how he was the one who journeyed to the lost lamb. And then there dawned the fantastic relief that swift and real repentance could get me right with him instantly! So he wonderfully revived my flagging spirit.

Peggy Buchanan has always considered it a very high priority to maintain regular daily devotions – although she is the first to say how difficult this is in certain seasons of life. When her children were small she was spurred on by the example of

> Susanna Wesley, who prayed with her pinafore thrown back over her head to signal to her family not to disturb her. She had seventeen children and a mainly absent husband with an itinerant ministry. How important this discipline is for a Christian leader's wife. Wherever we have lived I have always had a trysting place – usually a chair – where I seek God. My husband's strong faith and love for God has always been a constant source of inspiration to me.

For me, a more accessible approach to snatching opportune moments than that of Mrs Wesley is Anne Balfour's

> The real basic is finding time for God and me. This takes creativity – years ago, when *Playbus* came on (that dates me) I'd settle Alex in front of it and escape; quickly grabbing Bible, coffee (oh yes, and a cake). With the children older I got up earlier and later still the car became my regular holy space. Without 'me time', my emotional bank account overdraws until I almost get to gasping point before collapsing with relief in my favourite café; coffee mocha with whipped cream, jazz in the background and journal and pen in hand! Without that space – almost a diary appointment with me and God – everyone around me suffers, not just me, and I'm in no place to be Jesus to people, let alone hear his voice.

## Finding his rest

> Come to me, all you who are weary and burdened, and I will give you rest. Take my yoke upon you and learn from me, for I am gentle and humble in heart, and you will find rest for your souls. For my yoke is easy and my burden is light. (Mt. 11:28-30, NIV)

I hope never to lose sight of what a marvellous adventure it is to follow Jesus. The power of the gospel to save, to heal and transform is our reason for hope which motivates us in whatever work we take up, at every stage of life. But sometimes it isn't easy and these tender words of Jesus are so encouraging when I'm feeling overwhelmed with all there is to do. Eugene Petersen brings this familiar passage alive even more.

> Are you tired? Worn out? Burned out on religion? Come to me. Get away with me and you'll recover your life. I'll show you how to take real rest. Walk with me and work with me – watch how I do it. Learn the unforced rhythms of grace. I won't lay anything heavy or ill-fitting on you. Keep company with me and you'll learn to live freely and lightly.
> (Mt. 11:28-30, *The Message*)

Certainly, it is not unusual for those of us in leadership to become 'tired, worn out and burned out on religion' especially in a local church setting when each week rolls round with the same programme and the same people to pastor. There is a danger of becoming kind of professional Christians, but Jesus longs to lift the burdens from our shoulders and bring us into a pleasant place of rest and peace in the midst of busyness and pressure.

In the Old Testament, the word 'yoke' referred to something put upon us against our will – literally the wooden bar placed across the necks of oxen and other working animals and often a symbol of enemy oppression meted out by the Egyptians, Philistines or Babylonians. When the apostle Paul explains the liberty we have received from the power of sin, death and the devil he takes up this picture: 'It is for freedom that Christ has set us free. Stand firm, then, and do not let yourselves be burdened again by a yoke of slavery.' (Gal. 5:1, NIV) But sometimes in practice, being set free is easier said than done. Rather like the Galatian believers who were relying on their Jewish traditions maybe we can find ourselves weighed down with attitudes of guilt and self-sufficiency rather than walking freely with Jesus.

## 'The rucksack'

> A more contemporary image of a yoke struck me some years ago when our daughter was preparing for her Duke of Edinburgh's Award, which involved camping. Fearful of displeasing the PE teacher and anxious not to forget anything, Emma filled her enormous backpack with any items that might conceivably come in useful – along with the tent poles, cooking equipment, maps, clothes and compasses, food provisions and emergency supplies she insisted were necessary. When she put the rucksack on, its weight made her fall over. But she picked herself up again insisting adamantly that she could cope and Lyndon and I watched her stagger off with some concern!

Sometimes my life gets like that – I carry unnecessary burdens that tire me out. Many of us lug about bundles of guilt, unforgiveness, anxiety, resentments and sorrows from time to time like spiritual bag-ladies. And all along, God wants to take these weights from us so we can walk tall and enjoy all he has given to us.

> The weekend weather was foul and Emma arrived home absolutely exhausted, wet, frozen and starving. Dad lifted the rucksack from her aching shoulders and hugged the weary wanderer. We ran a bath, gave her a cup of tea and once she had recovered, listened to the stories of getting lost, trying to fry bacon in the rain, being chased

> by unfriendly cattle – and alas, after all this, that her group had failed to pass the test. Sharing her troubles helped enormously and by bedtime she was back to her normal cheerful self. The next day (because I am a mother) I tackled the pretty gruesome rucksack filled with muddled up muddy boots, squashed bananas and soggy bits of map. I threw a lot of stuff away, made a pile for washing and folded the rest up neatly, ready for next time – although I doubt there will be a next time.

Jesus washed his friends' feet and wants to do the same for us. Allowing him to remove the yoke of anxiety and failure brings such relief. When we are rested he sends us back out, entrusting us again with the mission and responsibilities that God has for us.

In the virtual rucksack I carry about there are items like guilt, resentment, fear, worry, pride and covetousness. Part of our spiritual discipline is to identify sins like these – for sin is what they are – and come to the Lord to be purified from them. In fact, there are a few references in the Bible to God purifying our hearts, but the main responsibility lies with us. 1 Peter 1 exhorts us: '… be holy in everything you do' (v. 15) and in verse 22, 'You were cleansed from your sins when you obeyed the truth, so now you must show sincere love to each other as brothers and sisters. Love each other deeply with all your heart.' (NLT) Loving isn't always easy in church life… When we humble ourselves and express our desire to be right the Holy Spirit comes to our aid.

One vicar's wife met with God as she reflected on her frustration and anger in the privacy of her car

> I was having a difficult day when my personal space and privacy had been severely threatened and decided I would write a letter of resignation. But to whom? As

> I was driving up the motorway I saw a hot air balloon high above me and began to think about the bigger picture seen from up there and reflected that God sees the bigger picture while I only see a part. I realised I need to attune myself with God in order not to lose his perspective.

Another lady confessed

> When everything we have to do and be is put together, it feels at times like we have a 15 ton weight on our shoulders. So much so, that the positives can be smothered.

Ellie Leighton has told her moving story in Chapter 10. In the midst of an intensely painful period of her life she found incredible peace in the presence of Jesus and the ability to forgive.

> Lined with avenues of blossoming cherry trees, the desert is not. But every so often, when the path has been at heights of barrenness, I've rounded a bend to be amazed by lush and fragrant meadows, watered by the sparkling and reviving waterfalls of the oasis. These are times when I've felt the Lord especially close, feeling his presence rather than just trusting through head knowledge – by an act of the will alone. Along the way he has showered on me diamonds of help and hope in many different guises, sometimes in the form of a new friend, an unexpected cheque when finances were desperate, a meal prepared for us at the end of a hectic day, and often in the form of books. *Total Forgiveness* by R.T. Kendall (Hodder and Stoughton, 2001) particularly helped me to avoid the pitfall of allowing resentment and bitterness to take root and develop a stranglehold on my life. It enabled me to move beyond the stalemate of plain 'not wanting to forgive'.

And there is one more piece of excess baggage we often carry – worry. The antidote to it is to pray

> Don't fret or worry. Instead of worrying, pray. Let petitions and praises shape your worries into prayers, letting God know your concerns. Before you know it, a sense of God's wholeness, everything coming together for good, will come and settle you down. It's wonderful what happens when Christ displaces worry at the center of your life. (Phil. 4:6,7 *The Message*)

I love that picture of shaping worries into prayers. It makes me imagine working with a hard lump of clay and being able to model it into something of value and gracefulness. Prayer changes things – I keep reminding myself – we can't afford not to talk to the Lord, in whatever way we can. So often we can be kept from prayer because of busyness, preoccupations and circumstances. It needs to become like a well-fitting garment we slip on as we walk in his presence, as we find the right balance between reverent fear and real freedom to be open and honest with our Father.

## Making it happen

So how can we find this closeness to Jesus and make it a reality, especially if the area of prayer has been one we feel we have failed with in the past?

Christine Freeland, who has moved to many places with the Methodist Church says

> In each location of our ministry I have asked for and been blessed with a prayer partner or triplet. They have come from different age groups, backgrounds, churches, but it has always been a 'partnership of equals' rather

than a 'counselling' situation. I cannot rate too highly the importance to me of this regular discipline of honest sharing, direct praying, checking progress .... in other words accountability. Having said that, I often find my prayer life consists of praying with my husband, with small groups in each of our churches, with various prayer initiatives – at the expense of my personal life of prayer which so easily becomes brief, formal and sometimes squeezed out altogether. The result is always spiritual dryness. I thank God for places where I can go from time to time to be alone with him.

Toki Miyashina, a Japanese Christian, wrote her own version of Psalm 23 – for busy people. It is worth stopping a moment to read it – perhaps out loud – reflecting on how easily our world can choke the spiritual life out of us.

The Lord is my pace-setter, I shall not rush.
He makes me stop and rest for quiet intervals:
He provides me with images of stillness, which restore my serenity.
He leads me in ways of efficiency through calmness of mind, and His guidance is peace.
Even though I have a great many things to accomplish each day, I will not fret, for His Presence is here:
His timelessness, His all-importance will keep me in balance.
He prepares refreshment in the midst of my activity, by anointing my mind with his oils of tranquillity. My cup of joyous energy overflows.
Surely harmony and effectiveness shall be the fruits of my hours,
for I shall walk in the pace of my Lord, and dwell in His house forever.
(Copyright K.H. Strange 1969. See www.mediachaplain.org/UK/inspiration)

## Some points to consider

1. Common sense is a great gift to apply to spiritual issues.

    - Are we realistic? Recognising the limitations we live with – not expecting too much of ourselves. Daily hour-long meditations are not a reasonable option for most of us.
    - Are we balanced? It's good to include each of the different components in prayer – ACTS (Adoration, Confession, Thanksgiving and Supplication).
    - Do we always pray within our faith and according to what touches our hearts? We may find it helpful to identify and focus on particular responsibilities and burdens God entrusts to us at a particular time rather than feel we have to pray about absolutely everything.
    - Are we real? Discovering what energises us helps us stick at it. Some are most at ease praying as they walk/iron/sit/drive. Is early morning best for prayer or some other point in the day?
    - Can you find prayer partners? Although time alone with God is vital, we gain in strength of faith when we join with others.

2. Creativity should be a hallmark of prayer – it is communication with God himself!

    - Is it boring? By approaching prayer times in different ways we can keep fresh. Spend the ten minutes it takes to drive somewhere to have a *thankfulness* session about an issue of concern. Then spend a few moments handing the situation to Jesus before turning off the ignition and getting on with the day.

- Can you bring in different things? Liturgy, Bible prayers, music, poetry, art… all feed our souls and spirits. Meditate on Scripture.
- Can you get ideas and input from other resources? There are scores of prayer diaries, websites, devotional books and guides, Bible study notes.
- Have you tried to keep a spiritual journal? When we write down some prayer requests and in a year's time turn back to see how God answered we will be encouraged. Journalling also logs our spiritual journey.
- Can you join with others in a variety of places? Prayer is not just a solitary activity.

3. Commitment

- It is important to acknowledge the importance of prayer.
- We can be wise and recognise where pitfalls may lie and be proactive (phone off, notepad to jot down important reminders like 'buy cornflakes' that come to distract the mind).
- Not easy, but facing up to guilt and other barriers keeping us from God's presence is vital. The longer we stay away the harder it feels to come back.
- Might it be worth considering becoming accountable to someone who will support and encourage us to develop our devotional disciplines? Perhaps we should seek out a spiritual director.

- Decide on what we are going to do – and do it. Perhaps for the moment that's only going to be a few slots in the week. Ask God to show us how we can practically put time aside.
- And when we fail, let us not feel condemned and give up!

# 13. Friends and Other Angels

'A friend is someone who understands your past, believes in your future and accepts you today the way you are.' I look for qualities of trust, reliability and confidentiality in a friend, someone I can be myself with. Proverbs 17:17 says 'A friend loves at ALL times'. And of course friendship means not only what we receive, but also what we give. (Anon)

## 'The geese'

Next autumn, when you see the geese heading south for the winter, flying along in a V shaped formation, you might consider what science has discovered as to why they fly that way. As each bird flaps its wings it creates uplift for the one immediately following. By flying in a V formation the whole flock adds at least 70% more to its flying range than if each bird was flying on its own.

When a goose falls out of formation it suddenly feels the drag and resistance of trying to go it alone and quickly gets back into place to take advantage of the lifting power of the bird in front.

When the leading goose gets tired it rotates back and another flies up front. It is sensible to take turns doing demanding jobs ... whether with people or with geese flying south. Geese honk from behind to encourage those up front to keep up their speed.

When a goose becomes sick or is injured by gunshot and falls out of formation, one or two of the others follow it down to lend help and protection. They stay with the wounded bird until it is able to fly or until it dies. Only then do they launch out again to catch up with their group.

People who share a common direction and a sense of community can get where they are going much more quickly and easily because they are travelling on the thrust of one another's efforts. If we have as much sense as a goose we will stay in formation with those who are headed the same way we are. If we have the sense of a goose, we will stand by each other when danger threatens or trouble comes.

(Author unknown)

This makes very good sense to me, and wherever genuine, loving unity is experienced it is wonderful to behold. These geese co-operate to reach a common destination, they recognise the weight that lies on the shoulders of the leaders and they take care of any who are weak and failing along the way. They communicate, actively encourage and are willing to wait for the right time to go forward – even if it wasn't as originally planned. What a picture of the body of Christ! How wonderful when it is a true portrait of our experience of the church.

## Churches together

In many cities, towns and districts unity among the church is alive and well. Sometimes large events – evangelistic missions, youth projects like London's 'Soul in the City' in the summer of 2004, or Alpha – mean that church leaders get together to pray and plan. This can lead to relationships of trust that make a world of difference when it comes to sharing responsibility and sharing real problems, joys and grief together. This happens fairly often for the actual leaders but it is rare for such fellowship to be extended to their wives, although in the situation described here, it really worked out

> For several years eight church leaders in our town, from all different denominations and some independent fellowships met together to pray, share together and organise events. Soon we began to meet monthly for family lunches and the wives' friendships also grew. We began getting together ourselves and it was a wonderful time of togetherness in the town. The support we gave each other was immeasurable, as there is nobody who understands better the stresses of ministry than another in the same situation. We became strong friends and though God has called all the other families to ministry elsewhere now we still keep in touch and appreciate all we had at that time.

## Ministering 'angels'

We all need friends of different kinds; where we live, work and worship – and further afield too. Describing how they most liked to relax, unsurprisingly – as many of us do tend to enjoy relaxing with those we can really trust – women returning our questionnaire said meeting up with friends who were nothing to do with the local church was very important. Rather than letting us struggle alone, God often sends help, sometimes even though we have neglected to ask him for it.

### Helen Clarke recalls early days in their ministry

As a mum with four small children I felt as though I was a prisoner to other peoples' pressures and expectations. In Chile we lived on the job, with the church meeting in our home, experiencing life in the goldfish bowl at its rawest. God sent a ministering angel into our situation. With the opportunity to be honest, in receiving wise help and expressing some of the fears and frustrations I experienced deep inner release through prayer ministry. This combined with some practical action gave me a fresh perspective on the situation, a healthier understanding of identity in Jesus and acceptance of my own limitations. How important it is for leaders and their spouses to have a safe place in which to be open and honest. That goes for our children too.

### Another mother, Julia Derbyshire, remembers with gratitude the support she received from unexpected sources on several occasions

We discovered, as a young couple about to move to our first pastorate, that there was nowhere for us to live. This was a concern, particularly as we had a ten-month-old baby. A couple in the church who had just been through the harrowing experience of dealing with a stillborn child opened their home to our little family. They welcomed not only us, but our healthy baby daughter, born just after theirs had died. Over the next two months we became as one family and, when the time came, it was difficult to leave. The love and generosity they showed taught me to enter into another's pain – I longed and prayed for her to bear a healthy child. My faith was strengthened when, some years later they held in their arms another baby daughter, completely healthy and today at university.

Living far from my own family took some adjusting. A single mum came alongside and became a surrogate aunt, babysitting my daughter whilst I enjoyed some much valued time out, secure in the knowledge that she loved going to 'Auntie Pauline's'.

As a young pastor's wife, living hundreds of miles from my own family and unable to see them very often, I remember being overwhelmed by the love of the church family who surprised me with an airplane ticket to visit my family. Someone had been concerned and spontaneously collected enough for me to go and enjoy a week away.

## Behind a mask

Many contributors to this book have highlighted the issue of having friends within the church fellowship. In years gone by, this was often frowned upon. The minister was expected to maintain the dignity of his position and if necessary stay aloof, separating his private life from the ministry. There was a perceived danger of having favourites and also the warning that relationships could develop in unhelpful, even disastrous, ways. So it was generally recommended for the pastor and his wife to keep behind a mask of evangelical probity and not let people into their private world. How has this changed?

Sally Thompsett writes

> Do we keep ourselves to ourselves or go out and make friends among the congregation? On one hand, being too cautious we could end up lonely, somewhat remote and thought of as deliberately holding ourselves aloof. On the other, we need to be wise about those we draw close to – careful to avoid the exclusivity tag and thoughtful about how much of our personal lives to share with others. There have been times when people have gossiped private information causing hurt and withdrawal.

In normal everyday life various people wear masks as a matter of routine. The surgeon's green gauze screens the vulnerable patient from infection, the welder's visor shields his face from harmful bright sparks and the actress's make-up, wig and costume hide her true identity to allow her to play a dramatic role effectively. And there is another kind of mask – which speaks to me of our relationship with God – the one that is lowered from above if ever the air pressure in an aeroplane changes. Being connected to an oxygen supply means we receive the life-giving breath we need for our own well-being, and once our own mask is securely fitted, we can assist others.

Apart from these very obvious, visible examples I believe wearing a mask is something most of us do anyway. Imagine how difficult it would be if everyone could read each other's minds! It is only common sense to filter our thoughts and feelings before we express ourselves openly. I am slowly learning to listen more than I speak after so many embarrassing experiences of 'putting my foot in it'. My opinion is often masked and sometimes I choose to say very much less than I might, or I put on a disguising smile – whether that is to protect others or to guard my own private world.

Many a minister's wife has learned to wear such a mask and in my opinion this is a good thing in moderation. It really doesn't do to let on how much our heart sinks whenever Mrs So-and-So moves into sight like a battleship ready to deliver yet another broadside of criticism and complaints. And living in a goldfish bowl, as many of us do, there may be times when we need to hide our personal worries from others. But what happens if the mask becomes a permanent fixture? As I have already mentioned, a recurring piece of advice from women sending back the questionnaire was 'Be yourself!' which suggests how especially important this is, but that when you are a minister's wife it isn't always easy.

Although in ministry we are called to share our lives with others in our church or organisation, there are times when it's wise to be careful about opening up to others. God can obviously provide us with trustworthy friends in any situation, within our own church or beyond it, but I have heard enough sad stories of broken relationships to suggest caution in this matter. It is a rare gift to find someone with whom we could share our deepest thoughts – that's one of the blessings of a strong, loving marriage – so without being too wary I believe we need to be tactful and discreet in our relationships with people in the church.

I met a young woman for whom this had all gone wrong. The experience crushed her and it may take time before she feels able to trust this particular group again. Caroline (not her real name) had only wanted to reach out in friendship and be a support to others. Thank God for the power of forgiveness and that he is able to bring blessing out of even the most dire circumstances – even if that might be years down the line.

> Caroline ran a women's group and she wanted to invite her close friend and prayer partner to be part of it. However, when this lady discovered that another certain person was in the group she freaked out. Taking Caroline aside, she told her many bad things about this individual's behaviour, accusing her of sexual impropriety – indeed, that she was trying to initiate an affair with her own husband! Everything blew up in Caroline's face as she was drawn into a wasps' nest of fierce anger, jealousy and deep pain. It ended with both women blaming her for things she hadn't done and spreading untrue rumours

among others in the church. 'I thought she was my friend, but that's all gone,' Caroline said. 'It's been a ghastly nightmare I never want to go through again.'

Painful experiences like this may lead a person to protect herself – with a mask of some kind. I have known minister's wives who have been so hurt that they no longer trust others and put up a front to prevent others from finding out who is inside. This might be OK in the short term but to live inside a persona on a permanent basis will inevitably lead to unhappiness and isolation. Another pastor's wife is likely to be the person most likely to understand and able to help anyone feeling in that predicament.

## Close friends

### Christine Freeland writes

Against all the advice from an older generation of ministers' wives I have found it essential to have close friendships with individuals and families in the church. Christian friendships include rather than exclude others and are the basis of community life. But of course there will be hurt when those we have trusted withdraw their friendship or a new appointment puts them beyond easy reach.

Even so, friendship is a must. I have especially valued the love and companionship of other ministers' wives – often from other denominations. Sometimes we need to seek each other out and just 'be there' for one another. Organised events for leaders' wives have often been valuable in making such introductions locally and in times of crisis it is good to provide a place of refuge for one another.

Christine Perkin agrees with this

> One of the most unhelpful things we were told when we were going into ministry was that we shouldn't form close friendships with our parishioners. We feel strongly that this is just wrong. We all need people around us with whom we can relate, have fun and share openly. To try and keep ourselves at a distance as if we don't have the same basic needs as everyone is totally unrealistic.
>
> In full-time ministry Paul and I don't have much free time to visit old friends and family – weekends are impossible and evenings often busy so we have found it all the more vital to make good friends wherever we are based. We need friends who are close by – not two hours up the M1! At each of our parishes we have formed a small group of just three or four couples with whom we have begun to feel close, and have met with for mutual support. Of course there is a risk involved here but the alternative is far worse – that we remain at a distance, slightly isolated and unable to share our real selves with our church family.
>
> Yes, we do have to choose carefully who to disclose certain things to, but that would be true whoever we were.

For the last two years Marion White, writing below, has met with four others, including me, for a 24-hour prayer retreat. We are all linked through long-term ministry at Spring Harvest. One of our number is Faith Forster; one of the first women to be recognised as a speaker who very much showed the way to those of us a few years younger coming behind her. These times have been so valuable – an opportunity for honest sharing and spiritual input among trusted friends. We would recommend it!

> Older, more mature Christians who understand the nature of our lifestyle and have struggled with some of the same

tensions and pressures are incredibly helpful. Sometimes to be at the end of the phone, or making time to visit, pray with and advise gives great support. It is often they who can alert us to any pitfalls or dangers they can see ahead of us which could be avoided.

## In this together

Living with Leadership was set up to link ministers' wives together. This it did, through large and small gatherings, the establishing of local groups and by modelling something – the 'safe place'. Relationships do not spring up overnight and they need to be nurtured and given the chance to share burdens and come under the load with love and prayer.

In the survey it emerged that leaders' wives generally feel unsupported and unprepared by their denominations and other structures. One Anglican wife said

> Although these (diocesan spouses) meetings sound positive they aren't much good! I feel they only pay lip service to being a support group but are actually quite shallow and I wouldn't ever dare to share what I was *really* feeling. Generally I find them incredibly frustrating but keep going in case things change.

Although many area groups work well the best ones come together because of a shared vision or purpose or need. I have been part of a local lunch group for about fifteen years. There are about seven or eight of us, based in local churches, Christian organisations, sitting on various local committees, and most of our children of the same age – many of them friends with each other too. We take it in turns to host a simple lunch, once or twice a term, and spend the time catching up and praying round the table for the needs we share. We all do our utmost not to miss it.

One group set up by Living with Leadership is in Manchester where Michele and Andy Hawthorne live with their two children. Andy heads Message Trust which through music and social projects reaches out to the city's young people. Michele had been in contact with other women who were married to Christian leaders in the area who all felt they needed 'something different'; so they set up 'Real' (We loved this name so much in Living with Leadership we called our newsletter *Real* as well!). The programme included all sorts of activities and events and continues to be really appreciated. This is Michele's take on it

> It's good to be yourself, not having to perform or live up to anyone's expectations, finding support and friendship with like-minded women. We pray when we meet but mix it in with a good laugh – and try to be a bit adventurous. We all feel more comfortable when we're enjoying something that really involves everybody. 'Real' began with an evening at a health club, with free use of the facilities – gym, swimming pool, sauna and steam – and then relaxing in a secluded corner of the bar. It's important to have daytime activities too so another time we went for a stroll through the woods to a country pub with open fires and delicious food. It's a good way to develop friendships. Then we went all creative with an arts and crafts evening – decorating frames, writing poetry and experimenting with clay. And at the end of the year we pull out all the stops with a meal, creating a lovely environment with fab food and a guest speaker and plenty of time for discussion over the coffee. We've got loads of other plans – God knows what will happen but we'll sure have fun trying to make it happen!

In the meantime New Wine has organised many excellent events for leaders' wives and other women in ministry. Anne Coles, who alongside Lindsay Melluish heads these, writes

> The New Wine vision is to equip local churches. As part of this we are aiming to support, minister to and re-envision the wife of the leader, since she is key to the leader's well-being and yet so often, the one who has no pastoral help. Of course one annual get-together cannot expect to fulfil this need; at best, it is only part of the picture.
>
> I am very aware that we need to make more use of our network to reach out during the year to the leaders' wives. However I'm also aware that most of them lead incredibly busy lives, often holding down part-time or even full-time jobs, as well as serving family and church.
>
> The important things are the opportunity to receive prayer ministry in a 'safe' place, the freedom to be real – cry and laugh(!), and the time to be able to focus on some really nourishing teaching.

This can actually happen very easily without all the paraphernalia. We can all pick up a phone and invite someone for a coffee. We're all in this together, our lives interlocking, sharing so many common experiences and needing each other's affirmation, support and friendship. Especially to be able to laugh together and have fun.

## Some points to consider

1. Are we mainly introvert or extrovert? In other words do people tend to drain or energise us? Probably some individuals are more draining than others.

2. Relationships come in all different shapes and sizes. It may be useful to write an 'inventory' of the *individuals* in our lives; attempting to summarise what each means to us and who we could call upon in various situations.
3. Are there *groups* of people we relate to? Do I receive the input I need to, for a balanced lifestyle?
4. Are there gaps in our relationships that we could pray about?
5. If there are strained or broken relationships, is there anything we can do to further necessary forgiveness and healing in them? Do we need help in this?

# Postscript

> Be merciful in action, kindly in heart, humble in mind. Accept life, and be most patient and tolerant with one another, always ready to forgive if you have a difference with anyone. Forgive as freely as the Lord has forgiven you. And, above everything else, be truly loving, for love is the golden chain of all the virtues.
>
> Let the peace of Christ rule in your hearts, remembering that as members of the same body you are called to live in harmony, and never forget to be thankful for what God has done for you.
>
> Let Christ's teaching live in your hearts, making you rich in the true wisdom. Teach and help one another along the right road with your psalms and hymns and Christian songs, singing God's praises with joyful hearts. And whatever you may have to do, do everything in the name of the Lord Jesus, thanking God the Father through him.
>
> (Col. 3:12–17, J.B. Phillips)

Having a leadership role in the church is a privilege and responsibility and I hope this book has served to encourage you, whatever your own situation. The two themes that seem to come through most strongly are; the call to discover the reality of God's faithfulness, and that *we* must be real ourselves. Knowing him, knowing ourselves.

We are called as his friends to serve him with full and generous hearts, knowing that whatever we do 'to the least of these' we do for Jesus. He alone fully understands the past and knows what the future holds. He loves us just as we are and longs to hold us close, especially in the hard times.

Those of us married to Christian leaders are 'in this together': with our husbands, the Lord and the church at large. The more we can support each other, building friendships – sharing in fun and laughter, trials and tears – the better. I believe our lives are interwoven in many ways and at many levels.

As I was putting together these last pages this morning, I received this email from Sheila Shersby which really made me smile!

> I've just been having a sort through some old papers today and came across a letter I thought I'd share with you. It was written to me on 13 March 1972 by George Reindorp, the then Bishop of Guildford, following my engagement to Brian, who was then a curate in my local church. It reads as follows:
>
> *My dear Sheila*
>
> *So you're going to join the uncanonised saints! Many congratulations.*
>
> *You'll have to cope with the world, the flesh and the parish: and at times you will want to murder the lot. But all your married life as a parson's wife you'll have a host of friends.*
>
> *But remember you're marrying Brian* not *'The Reverend' Brian: and certainly not the curate of Stoughton.*
>
> *So love him and laugh at him.*
>
> *Sincerely*
>
> *George Guildford*

# Appendix 1

## *We're in this together* – questionnaire for Christian leaders' wives

### The facts, figures and statistics

Questionnaires were sent to about 2,500 women, and 458 completed and returned them (a response rate of 18 per cent). Information was given anonymously and treated with confidentiality. I am very grateful to all those who replied as I believe that this research gives authenticity to the content of this book, making it more helpful to leaders' wives and those who seek to nurture them.

The questionnaire is reproduced below with the response summaries and, where appropriate, percentages (rounded off to the nearest whole number). Sometimes questions were unanswered so the figures (and percentages) are usually based on the actual responses. In the case of multiple answers the percentages are based on the total number of questionnaires returned. Not all the details have been included here. The full results are too long and complicated to be written in this appendix.

## A. About you (please tick appropriate boxes)

### 1. How old are you?

| | | |
|---|---|---|
| 20–24 | 2 | 0.5% |
| 25–29 | 10 | 2% |
| 30–39 | 100 | 22% |
| 40–49 | 159 | 35% |
| 50–59 | 139 | 30.5% |
| Over 60 | 47 | 10% |
| Total | 457 | 100% |

### 2. How many years have you been in the ministry?

| | | |
|---|---|---|
| under 2 | 21 | 5% |
| 3–5 | 39 | 9% |
| 6–9 | 65 | 14% |
| 10–24 | 228 | 51% |
| 25 or more | 96 | 21% |
| Total | 449 | 100% |

### 3. How old were you when you married?

| | | |
|---|---|---|
| 20–24 | 247 | 54% |
| 25–29 | 148 | 33% |
| 30–39 | 48 | 10% |
| 40–49 | 7 | 2% |
| 50–59 | 4 | 1% |
| Total | 454 | 100% |

### 4. When did your husband start his ministry?

| | | |
|---|---|---|
| Before we married | 119 | 26% |
| After we married | 333 | 74% |
| Total | 452 | 100% |

**5. How old were you when he started his ministry?**

| | | |
|---|---|---|
| 20–24 | 108 | 24% |
| 25–29 | 153 | 34% |
| 30–39 | 140 | 31% |
| 40–49 | 38 | 9% |
| 50–59 | 6 | 1.5% |
| Over 60 | 2 | 0.5% |
| Total | 447 | 100% |

## B. Where you live

| | | |
|---|---|---|
| 6. England: | | |
| North West | 36 | 8% |
| North East | 29 | 6% |
| Yorkshire | 55 | 12% |
| East Midlands | 15 | 3% |
| West Midlands | 14 | 3% |
| East Anglia | 13 | 2% |
| South East | 103 | 23% |
| Greater London | 73 | 17% |
| South West | 49 | 11% |
| Scotland | 16 | 3.5% |
| N. Ireland | 31 | 7% |
| Wales | 17 | 3.5% |
| Other | 5 | 1% |
| Total | 456 | 100% |

**7. What kind of area are you in?**

| | | |
|---|---|---|
| Rural | 69 | 15% |
| Small town | 105 | 23% |
| Large town | 87 | 19% |
| City centre | 58 | 13% |
| City suburbs | 105 | 23% |
| Council estate | 31 | 7% |
| Total | 455 | 100% |

**8. What is your accommodation?**

| | | |
|---|---|---|
| Small flat | 4 | 1% |
| Large flat | 4 | 1% |
| Average house | 209 | 46% |
| Large house | 215 | 47% |
| Other (please state) | | |
| House | 13 | 3% |
| Small house | 4 | 1% |
| Bungalow | 3 | 0.5% |
| Other | 2 | 0.5% |
| Total | 454 | 100% |

**9. Who owns it?**

| | | |
|---|---|---|
| We do | 136 | 30% |
| Church/agency | 307 | 57% |
| It is rented | 12 | 13% |
| Total | 455 | 100% |

10. **Where is it located?** answer either a) or b)

a) if you are in church ministry:

| | | |
|---|---|---|
| very close to the church | 135 | 33% |
| nearby | 216 | 53% |
| not near at all | 56 | 14% |
| Total | 407 | 100% |

b) if you are in parachurch ministry:

| | | |
|---|---|---|
| on agency property | 8 | 22% |
| where we choose | 28 | 78% |
| Total | 36 | 100% |

11. **Is your home regularly used for church ministry?**

| | | |
|---|---|---|
| Yes | 342 | 75% |
| No | 116 | 25% |
| Total | 458 | 100% |

**If 'yes' please describe in what ways it is used:**

(342 individuals responded as follows)

| | |
|---|---|
| Business/leadership meetings | 246 |
| Hospitality/catering | 129 |
| 'Ministry' group meetings | 152 |
| Counselling/pastoral care | 99 |
| Office/study | 62 |
| Youth/children's work | 57 |
| Prayer meetings | 48 |
| Other | 39 |

## C. Ministry

**12. Is your ministry primarily in:**

| | | |
|---|---|---|
| Local church | 354 | 88% |
| Wider church | 26 | 7% |
| Parachurch agency | 20 | 5% |
| Total | 400 | 100% |

**13. What denomination are you?**

| | | |
|---|---|---|
| Anglican | 203 | 45% |
| Baptist | 77 | 17% |
| Methodist | 33 | 7% |
| New Church | 39 | 8.5% |
| Pentecostal | 35 | 7.5% |
| Presbyterian | 31 | 7% |
| Other | 36 | 8% |
| Total | 454 | 100% |

**14. Which of these describes your husband's ministry?** (tick all that apply)

| | |
|---|---|
| Associate or assistant | 46 |
| Evangelist | 96 |
| In charge of a church | 340 |
| In training | 24 |
| Leadership in parachurch organisation | 22 |
| Missionary | 19 |
| Musician | 48 |
| Pastoral care | 237 |
| Preacher | 284 |
| Regional or national leadership | 67 |
| Retired | 12 |

| | |
|---|---|
| Teaching or training | 148 |
| Writer/academic | 33 |
| Other | 52 |
| Total | 1428 |

15. **What role do you have in relation to your husband's ministry?**

(Total number of individuals replying – 386)

| | |
|---|---|
| Supporting | 253 |
| Shared leadership | 41 |
| Own separate ministry | 45 |
| Other | 47 |

16. **Please describe your main occupation(s)**

(Total number of individuals replying – 436)

(n.b. some are now retired)

| | |
|---|---|
| Homemaker/wife/mother | 148 |
| In education | 103 |
| Christian ministry | 42 |
| Administration/finance/ secretarial | 37 |
| Allied Healthcare profession | 34 |
| Nursing | 23 |
| Social work and law | 19 |
| Carer | 17 |
| Management/executive | 15 |
| Medical profession | 11 |
| Counsellor/therapist | 11 |
| Artist/musician etc. | 8 |
| Student | 6 |
| Other | 17 |

17. **What do you consider are your principal strengths and gifts?**

(Total number of individuals replying – 423)

| | |
|---|---|
| Organisation/administration | 101 |
| Hospitality | 94 |
| Encouragement and helping | 93 |
| Leadership/teaching | 92 |
| Caring | 89 |
| Counselling/listening | 80 |
| Worship/music | 57 |
| Prayer/prophetic | 49 |
| Working with children and youth | 32 |
| Creativity | 30 |
| Communication | 30 |

18. **In which of the following church (or parachurch related) activities are you involved – as a leader or as part of a team?** (tick all that apply)

(Total number of individuals replying – 442)

| | |
|---|---|
| Hospitality | 330 |
| Prayer | 272 |
| Women's groups | 204 |
| Children's work | 204 |
| Catering | 180 |
| Counselling | 175 |
| Running events | 167 |
| Visiting | 164 |
| Speaking | 158 |
| Worship | 151 |
| Administration | 148 |
| In the community | 139 |

| | |
|---|---|
| Evangelism | 108 |
| Vision, strategy | 102 |
| Youth | 101 |
| Decoration/artistic | 89 |
| Preschool groups | 92 |
| Crèche | 83 |
| Writing | 55 |

19. **What preparation, training and support have you received to help you in your role of leader's wife?**

(Total number of individuals replying – 387)

| | |
|---|---|
| Very little or none at all | 81 |
| Nothing formal – learned 'on the job' | 37 |
| Some during own or husband's training | 96 |
| Through conferences/short courses | 68 |
| From other training and work experience | 35 |
| Personal study | 13 |
| Mentoring relationships | 24 |
| Local support from groups/ individuals | 33 |

20. **If you and your husband work together, how do you describe this partnership?**

(Total number of individuals replying – 331)

| | |
|---|---|
| Good | 130 |
| Difficult/challenging | 48 |
| 'OK' | 32 |

| | |
|---|---|
| We don't work together | 26 |
| We're simply 'just married' | 73 |
| It's a co-partnership | 47 |
| We complement each other | 71 |

21. **When and how did you become aware that God was leading you into ministry as a couple?**

(Total number of individuals replying – 395)

| | |
|---|---|
| Before we met | 90 |
| Called separately | 79 |
| During courtship/engagement period | 253 |
| Post marriage | 74 |
| No definite sense of calling | 11 |

22. **Can you point to an experience or growing recognition of God's call to you as an individual?**

(Total number of individuals replying – 279)

| | |
|---|---|
| Through prophetic word/scripture/prayer | 41 |
| At an event or through significant life experience | 29 |
| Had a strong inner certainty | 114 |
| Challenge for others | 9 |
| Growing gradual awareness | 86 |

23. **What is the greatest challenge to you in your role?**

(Total number of individuals replying – 410)

| | |
|---|---|
| Finding the right balance in our lives | 149 |

| | |
|---|---|
| Living with others' expectations | 63 |
| Coping with criticism/rejection/ church problems | 46 |
| Prioritising what to do | 45 |
| Walking close to God | 34 |
| Being myself | 30 |
| Getting through the workload | 32 |
| Having enough time with husband | 26 |
| Finding friends and support | 23 |
| Saying 'no'! | 17 |
| Adjusting | 11 |

## D. Family

**24. Do you have children?**

| | | |
|---|---|---|
| No | 21 | 5% |
| Yes | 432 | 95% |
| Total | 453 | 100% |

The children's ages ranged from 'on the way' to adult. The numbers of children in each family reported are:

| | | |
|---|---|---|
| 1 child | 32 | 8% |
| 2 children | 183 | 44% |
| 3 children | 140 | 33% |
| 4 children | 52 | 12% |
| 5 children or more | 13 | 3% |
| Total | 453 | 100% |

**25. Do any of them have any kind of special needs?**

| | | |
|---|---|---|
| No | 388 | 85% |
| Yes | 70 | 15% |
| Total | 458 | 100% |

*(please describe briefly)*

| | |
|---|---|
| Learning difficulties (including 19 with dyslexia) | 25 |
| Serious medical problems | 16 |
| Autism and similar conditions | 12 |
| Emotional/behavioural problems | 11 |
| Mental health problems | 6 |
| Giftedness | 4 |
| Speech/language difficulties | 3 |
| Learning disabilities | 2 |

**26. How do you think your ministry lifestyle affects them?**

(Total number of individuals replying – 392)

| | |
|---|---|
| Children have left home now | 54 |
| It has been generally positive | 82 |
| Enriched by meeting people and church family | 54 |
| It has strengthened their faith | 39 |
| It has made them confident/sociable/caring | 25 |
| They see more of Dad in daytime | 14 |
| They don't see enough of us (esp. Dad) | 47 |
| See church life intrusive and causing stress | 43 |
| Felt under pressure to behave in certain ways | 29 |

| | |
|---|---|
| Affected by moving | 27 |
| Problems at school (e.g. bullying) | 14 |
| Missed out financially | 9 |

27. **How do you make sure to have 'family time'?**

(Total number of individuals replying – 436)

| | |
|---|---|
| Guard days off | 111 |
| Eat together regularly | 110 |
| Holidays | 44 |
| Plan well ahead | 42 |
| Saturday for the family | 34 |
| Do things together | 32 |
| It is really difficult | 30 |
| Special family time and traditions | 25 |
| Sunday lunch | 23 |
| Control the telephone | 14 |
| Get away from church/home | 12 |

28. **What do you pray and wish for most in your marriage and family life?**

(Total number of individuals replying – 408)

| | |
|---|---|
| Children to grow in their faith | 213 |
| Children to come to or return to Christ | 126 |
| Continued strong godly marriage | 233 |
| Closeness as a family | 98 |
| Balance and privacy | 32 |
| Continued health and serve God till old! | 45 |

## E. Real life issues

29. **Have any of the following been serious issues for you?** (tick all that apply)

| | | |
|---|---|---|
| Accommodation problems | 102 | 22% |
| Church's unrealistic expectation | 120 | 26% |
| Crisis of own faith | 65 | 14% |
| Criticism of husband or the church | 216 | 47% |
| Feeling isolated | 255 | 56% |
| Financial needs | 166 | 36% |
| Lack of training/preparation | 98 | 21% |
| Marriage difficulties | 82 | 18% |
| Not sure of my role | 154 | 34% |
| Physical or mental illness | 119 | 26% |
| Safety of you and your family | 46 | 10% |
| Serious problems with children | 51 | 11% |
| Work overload | 269 | 59% |
| Other (please state) | 66 | 14% |
| Total number of responses | 458 | |

Please explain further if you wish:

30. **Would you describe yourself as 'stressed':**

| | | |
|---|---|---|
| Constantly | 14 | 4% |
| Regularly | 132 | 33% |
| Occasionally | 223 | 57% |
| Almost never | 25 | 6% |
| Total | 394 | 100% |

31. **From where do you draw spiritual strength?** (tick all that apply)

| | | |
|---|---|---|
| Personal devotional times | 317 | 69% |
| Husband or other individual | 285 | 62% |

| | | |
|---|---|---|
| Church services | 241 | 53% |
| Conferences/retreats | 226 | 49% |
| Cell or friendship group | 187 | 41% |
| Ministry and worship tapes | 159 | 35% |
| Prayer group | 98 | 21% |
| Special events | 95 | 21% |
| Other (please describe) | 102 | 22% |
| Total number of responses | 458 | |

32. **Where do you go and what do you do to relax and just 'be yourself'?**

(Total number of individuals replying – 438)

| | |
|---|---|
| Walk | 152 |
| (With dog) | (22) |
| Gym/sport/swim | 123 |
| Time with friends and family | 117 |
| Read | 76 |
| Holidays and days out | 63 |
| Garden | 59 |
| Art/craft/creative | 56 |
| Music | 38 |
| Cinema/theatre/cultural | 32 |
| Meals out with husband or close friends | 26 |
| Shopping | 20 |
| Pub/coffee shop | 17 |
| Devotional/worship | 13 |
| Go to work | 12 |
| Study | 10 |

33. **Do you meet with other women married to Christian leaders?** (please tell us about this)

| | | |
|---|---|---|
| No | 126 | 29% |
| Very rarely | 4 | 1% |

| | | |
|---|---|---|
| Rarely | 12 | 3% |
| Very occasionally | 6 | 1% |
| Occasionally | 83 | 19% |
| Not often | 8 | 2% |
| Yes | 199 | 45% |
| Total | 438 | 100% |

34. **What do you most value and enjoy about being married to a Christian leader?**

(Total number of individuals replying – 421)

| | |
|---|---|
| Him! | 57 |
| Sharing in partnership with him | 85 |
| Personal fulfilment | 78 |
| Privilege of seeing God at work | 66 |
| Being part of the church | 63 |
| Working with people | 62 |
| Friendships it leads to | 20 |
| Freedom and flexibility | 15 |
| Not much – if anything | 11 |

35. **What positive suggestions would you pass on to others in a similar position?**

(Total number of individuals replying – 391)

| | |
|---|---|
| Make your marriage a priority | 57 |
| Be yourself and take care of yourself | 167 |
| Find a good friend (or friends) | 89 |
| Be ruthless – only do what God is asking | 65 |
| Be sure to take proper time off | 84 |
| Stay close to God | 76 |

# Appendix 2

## Putting on a local event for fellow leaders' wives

In the past Living with Leadership organised special evenings, lunches and whole days tailored for women married to local church leaders and others in ministry. This was especially successful in areas where there was already a strong unity between the different denominations; where leaders met together for prayer, encouragement and to plan joint projects. In several areas these groups continue and maybe you would like to do something that could work well in your area and perhaps include women in leadership who are single or whose husbands work in other jobs.

The following suggestions and questions may help.

### Form a planning group

- Have three or more of you, from different churches or ministries in the locality. Where possible build on existing relationships.
- The group probably needs to meet about three times before the event and once afterwards. It is important to have time to pray together and develop friendship.

- Delegate responsibilities – catering, venue, mailing and other admin, finance, programme, follow-up would be areas to include.

## Decide on the nature of event

- What do you hope to achieve and how much time and energy can you give to it? What will it include?
- Which time of year, day of the week, time?
- How long? Start and finish times?
- How wide is your catchment area?
- How many do you expect?
- Who will speak (if anyone)?
- What refreshments will you offer?

## Venue

- Friendly and comfortable ambiance (is it warm enough?)
- Accessible and easy to find. Easy parking.
- Will it help to include travel instructions and a map with invitation?

## Finance and administration

- Is there a budget? How will you finance the event?
- How will you create an invitation mailing list?
- What will need organising on the day (registration, labels etc.)

## Invitation mailing

- Timing should give about six weeks notice before the event.
- Consider what to include:
  1. Mail merged (if possible) letter, signed by you (first name signature scanned into computer) with other names of planning group representing a range of denominations at the bottom.
  2. A5 invitation card that may be put up somewhere at home – may act as a reminder!
  3. Suggestion that they also invite a friend (also in ministry).
  4. Response slip.

## Managing responses

- How will you know who is coming? Consider confirmation that you know they are coming – by email or phone call – especially if it is more than an informal coffee; a meal or a whole day.

## Catering

- Keep it as simple as possible but add 'special touches'.
- Provide for those with special dietary needs.
- Label desserts.

## Programme

- Keep the aims before you as you plan the time.
- Ensure there is ample time (50 per cent of the whole?) when they can just talk together. This can include discussion groups.
- Consider whether you will include worship. Bear in mind the denominational spread and select well-known songs. Provide words. Keep it short, the purpose mainly being to seek a relaxed atmosphere in God's presence. For some more 'social' events worship may not be appropriate.
- Offer the opportunity for prayer, including one-to-one with the speaker or organisers if desired. Stress the concept of this being a 'safe place' where confidentiality is respected.
- Consider whether you could give them a small gift as they leave. (Handmade bookmark, flower, small freebie from Body Shop or wherever – worth asking!)

## Follow up and future plans

- Ask them to fill in a feedback form to help you assess what is really wanted. This may guide you as you plan future meetings.
- Small informal friendship groups may spring out of this event. These cannot be engineered – some work, others fold after a time. If you give everyone expressing an interest in a group each others' names etc. (get permission first!) probably best to leave them to arrange something themselves.
- If possible at the event give them the date and details of the next planned meeting to put in their diaries.

# Appendix 3

*Lifestyle Inventory* (adapted from 'Holmes/ Rahe Social Readjustment Rating Scale' Journal of Psychosomatic Research, Vol. 11, 1967)

In the column provided note the value of each event which has happened to you during the previous year. Add the individual scores to ascertain your stress rating.

| *Life Event* | *Rating* | *Your Score* |
|---|---|---|
| 1. Death of spouse | 100 | |
| 2. Divorce | 73 | |
| 3. Marital separation | 65 | |
| 4. Death of close family member | 63 | |
| 5. Major personal injury or illness | 53 | |
| 6. Marriage | 50 | |
| 7. Losing your job | 47 | |
| 8. Marital reconciliation | 45 | |
| 9. Retirement from work | 45 | |
| 10. Major change in health or behaviour of family member | 44 | |
| 11. Pregnancy | 40 | |
| 12. Sexual difficulties | 39 | |
| 13. Gaining a new family member | 39 | |
| 14. Major business readjustment | 39 | |

| *Life Event* | *Rating* | *Your Score* |
|---|---|---|
| 15. Major change in financial state | 38 | |
| 16. Death of a close friend | 37 | |
| 17. Changing to a different line of work | 36 | |
| 18. Major change in amount of arguments with spouse | 35 | |
| 19. Taking on a mortgage or loan greater than £40,000 | 31 | |
| 20. Major change in responsibilities at work | 29 | |
| 21. Son or daughter leaving home | 29 | |
| 22. In-law troubles | 29 | |
| 23. Outstanding personal achievement | 28 | |
| 24. Spouse beginning or ceasing work outside the home | 26 | |
| 25. Major change in living conditions | 25 | |
| 26. Revision of personal habits | 24 | |
| 27. Troubles with boss | 23 | |
| 28. Major changes in working hours or conditions | 20 | |
| 29. Change of residence | 20 | |
| 30. Major change in usual type and/or amount of recreation | 19 | |
| 31. Major change in church activities | 19 | |
| 32. Major change in social activities | 18 | |
| 33. Taking on mortgage or loan of less than £40,000 | 17 | |
| 34. Major change in sleeping habits | 16 | |
| 35. Major change in eating habits | 15 | |
| 36. Holiday | 13 | |
| 37. Christmas | 12 | |
| 38. Minor violations of the law | 11 | |

## Total

Up to 150 – you have a low amount of life change and a low susceptibility to stress-induced health breakdown.

150–300 – You have a 50% chance of a major health breakdown in the next two years.

300+ – You have an 80% chance of a major health breakdown in the next two years.

# Real Lives

D.J. Carswell

"You are on a train; you look at the people around you. Someone hides behind a newspaper. Another dozes; a young man nods to the beat from his Discman. A baby cries further along the carriage and a table of football fans celebrate an away victory over a few cans of lager. Someone's mobile goes off; a student sitting next to you sends a text message. Eavesdropping on the conversations you catch soundbites from those around you. Who exactly are they, you wonder?"

Real people.
All different
Everyone with a life story.
Real lives.

In *Real Lives* you will meet, among others...a famous footballer...a sophisticated lady from South Africa...an Olympic athlete...a backpacker exploring the States...a Brahmin from India...a young, abused girl...the greatest man in history who was a child refugee...and the author's own story of a changed life.

ISBN: 1-85078-412-4

Available online or from your local Christian bookshop

# True Grit

## Deborah Meroff

A wake-up call to crises facing women around the world, told through the exciting stories of nine courageous people and hard-hitting 'Vital Statistics' files.

This tells the inspiring true adventures of nine 'ordinary' women who are making a difference in such places as Tajikistan, India and Lebanon. We hear about Kathryn, a deaf American who built a ministry to the deaf in Israel; Pam, who lived and worked in war-racked Tajikstan, a country completely alien and unknown to Westerners; and Cindy who ended up returning as a missionary to Vietnam, a country from which she had had a dangerous escape as a teenager.

Fact files between stories highlight global female abuse, such as child brides, sex trafficking, girl soldiers and 'honour' killings. But the book does not stop there. *True Grit* goes on to point out simple ways for all of us to help turn the tide for women worldwide.

**Deborah Meroff** has travelled to over eighty countries in the last eighteen years in her role of journalist-at-large for the mission organisation, Operation Mobilisation. She has written several books, plus dozens of articles in several countries and is a columnist for *Woman Alive* magazine.

ISBN: 1-85078-575-9

Available online or from your local Christian bookshop

# Turning Points

## Vaughan Roberts

Is there meaning to life?
Is human history a random process going nowhere?
Or is it under control – heading towards a goal, a destination?
And what about my life? Where do I fit into the grand scheme of things?

These are topical questions in any age, but perhaps particularly so in a largely disillusioned postmodern era such as ours. Vaughan Roberts addresses these questions and others as he looks at what the Bible presents as the 'turning points' in history, from creation to the end of the world.

This book does not read like a normal history book. No mention is made of great battles and emperors of whom we learnt at school. It will not help you pass exams or score extra marks in a pub quiz.

It aims to do something far more important, to help you see history as God sees it, so that you might fit in with his plans for the world.

'Racy and profound, brilliant and biblical, this book is a powerful apologetic and magnet to Jesus Christ.' **Michael Green, Adviser in Evangelism to the Archbishops of Canterbury and York**

**Vaughan Roberts** is Rector of St Ebbe's Church, Oxford. He has worked extensively with students and is a frequent speaker at University Christian Unions, and at conventions such as Word Alive and Keswick. He is a keen sportsman.

ISBN: 1-85078-336-5

Available online or from your local Christian bookshop